Changes

Readings for ESL Writers

Changes

Readings for ESL Writers

Jean Withrow
Borough of Manhattan Community College
City University of New York

Gay Brookes
Borough of Manhattan Community College
City University of New York

Martha Clark Cummings
LaGuardia Community College, City University of New York

ST. MARTIN'S PRESS
New York

Editor: Kathleen Keller
Development editor: Andrea Guidoboni
Project editor: Elise Bauman
Editorial assistant: Robert Skiena
Production supervisor: Alan Fischer
Text design: Leon Bolognese & Associates, Inc.
Cover design: Darby Downey

ACKNOWLEDGMENTS

Page 2, Cruz, Melba, "Leaving Home Behind," Melba Cruz, *ESL Voices: Selections from ESL Students' Writing.* New York: Department of Development Skills, Borough of Manhattan Community College, CUNY, June 1988.

Page 4, Chan, Iu-Choi, "Freedom," by Iu-Choi Chan, first printed in *Patterns Plus,* p. 20, Houghton Mifflin; 1988. Reprinted by permission of the author.

Page 5, Monestime, Bernadin, "At Sea." Reprinted by permission of the author.

Page 8, Kincaid, Jamaica, Selections from "A Walk to the Jetty" from *Annie John* by Jamaica Kincaid. Copyright © 1983, 1984, 1985 by Jamaica Kincaid. Reprinted by permission of Farrar, Strauss & Giroux, Inc.

Page 16, Zongren, Liu. "To the Melting Pot" and "My Way or Theirs" from *Two Years in the Melting Pot.* Copyright 1988 by Liu Zongren. Published by China Books & Periodicals, 2929 24th Street, San Francisco, CA 94110. Revised edition 1988. First published September, 1984; reprinted in 1985, 1986, 1987.

Page 21, Sheehy, Gail, "Worlds to Go before I Sleep," pp. 192–197, from *Spirit of Survival* by Gail Sheehy. Text copyright © Gail Sheehy. By permission of William Morrow & Co., Inc.

Page 29, Reid, Alastair. Excerpted from *Whereabouts,* "Notes on Being a Foreigner," copyright © 1987 by Alastair Reid. Published by North Point Press and reprinted by permission of North Point Press.

Page 33, Frost, Robert, "Stopping by Woods on a Snowy Evening." Copyright 1923 by Holt, Rinehart and Winston and renewed 1951 by Robert Frost. Reprinted from *The Poetry of Robert Frost,* edited by Edward Connery Lathem, by permission of Henry Holt & Co.

Page 34, Ramírez, Armando Socarras, "Stowaway." Reprinted with permission from the January 1970 *Reader's Digest.* Copyright © 1969 by Reader's Digest Association, Inc.

Page 38, Kingston, Maxine Hong. "Moon Orchid's Arrival" from *The Woman Warrior: Memories of a Girlhood Among Ghosts* by Maxine Hong Kingston. Copyright © 1975, 1976, by Maxine Hong Kingston. Reprinted by permission of Alfred A. Knopf, Inc.

Page 46, Mok, Maggie, "Sometimes Home Is Not Really Home." Reprinted by permission of the author.

Acknowledgments and copyrights are continued at the back of the book on pages 226–27, which constitute an extension of the copyright page.

To our mothers and to the memory of our fathers

Preface: To the Instructor

Changes: Readings for ESL Writers is an interactive, developmental, and integrated skills book focusing on reading and writing. It is intended for adults at intermediate to advanced levels. The book helps ESL students develop all language skills, especially reading and writing, through reading and responding to selections in writing and through talking with their peers. This leads to more writing, which is then shared with their peers and instructor.

The book offers a choice of 34 readings with related activities and 18 extra readings, bringing the total to 52. The readings are grouped around themes that fit under the larger heading of *changes*. Before and after each reading are a number of activities to choose from. These activities draw upon all language skills. The extra readings at the end of each unit focus on the same themes but have no accompanying activities, thus allowing you and your students the freedom to use any of the readings in any way you choose.

Changes contains certain features that make it unique among other reading/writing texts:

- The readings, which encompass a variety of genres, voices, and moods, include stories, poems, essays, letters, myths, and folktales.
- The readings vary in length and level of difficulty.
- All readings are original, not adapted.
- The writers, both professional and student, represent many different nationalities.
- The activities are stimulating, thought-provoking, and student-centered.
- Most activities are structured for collaborating and sharing in small groups, in pairs, or in whole-class discussions.
- The varied readings and activities allow for instructor and student choice.

The activities combine reading and writing in unique ways. Students progress from reading to recording the significance of the text for themselves in reading logs. Then, because reading and writing are seen as social events taking place in a community, students are asked to talk in collaborative groups in order to understand the significance of the text for others. Class discussion helps shape many diverse understandings into a common meaning (or meanings). Finally, students write once again, this time with a new context for their thoughts and understandings. Reading and writing are further connected as processes through activities that aim at raising students' awareness of reading/writing strategies.

The text is based on the theory that the meaning of a text is constructed through interaction with text and peers, and that this meaning changes and develops with further interaction as the reader sees the subject from different viewpoints, as expressed in further reading, or in the writings and thoughts of peers. Meaning resides as much in the reader as in the text itself. This view of the act of reading shapes the categories and nature of the activities in the text.

Changes is also based on our understanding of the writing process and its development in ESL students. We know the writing process is a complex linguistic and cognitive one where thought and language interact in increasingly abstract ways. It is also fluid and open ended. The development of certain abilities in the process is gradual and, yet, ungradable. These understandings inform our approach to teaching writing.

This text does not take students through all steps of the writing process, commonly defined as prewriting, revision, and editing. Rather, it concentrates on the early stages of the writing process: gathering ideas, rehearsing them, and getting started. The writing activities may seem loose and unfinished, but they are structured in a pointedly interactive way.

Of course, you may wish to spend more time on the later stages of the writing process than the book specifically does. Although we do not spell it out, you will see many places in the text where students can be encouraged to revise and edit their writing further.

In this student-centered text, the role of the instructor is often implied. Some of your tasks will include the following:

- setting up groups or pairs
- answering questions about the activities, the reading, the instructions for writing
- structuring and facilitating class discussion and sharing, helping to make sense and order out of the sometimes conflicting and disordered group reports
- adding the interpretations of the larger community

One thing to remember is that we don't think there are right and wrong answers, responses, or interpretations to the readings or to students' responses and writings. We hope you will do what is necessary to stimulate the construction and reconstruction of interpretations and the composition of students' own thoughts on self-selected topics. To this end, you may prod and encourage, suggest and question. But primarily we hope you will structure a student-centered classroom with appropriate interaction to provide a positive, tolerant, and supportive atmosphere for students' expression of honest feelings, questions, tentative propositions, and responses to what they read and to one another.

This book is the product of collaboration. We would like to thank those who have collaborated with us, knowingly or unknowingly, and to put forth their names for your appreciation. First, we thank our students, who taught us how to teach, especially those who tried out sections of the text and gave us feedback. Second, we thank the many authors whose works appear in the book and who write, in a sense, on our behalf. Third, we thank our teachers who gave of their wisdom: Ann Berthoff, Ken Bruffee, Peter Elbow, Caleb Gattegno, and Donald Murray, among many others whose ideas shine through *Changes*. Fourth, we thank our colleagues who shared their ideas about students and teaching, especially those we've interviewed and observed. Another group of colleagues who gave us valuable feedback and encouragement are our reviewers: Lynn Goldstein, Monterey Institute of International Studies; Jann Huizenga, LaGuardia Community College; Stan Jones, Carleton University; Alexandra Krapels, University of South Carolina; Marjorie Knowles, San Joaquin Delta College; Joanne Leibman, University of Arkansas; Martha Low, Oregon State University; Denise Murray, San Jose State University; Tony Silva, Purdue University; and Stephen Thewlis, San Francisco State. Finally, we thank the St. Martin's editors and staff for their great assistance and support: Susan Anker; Andrea Guidoboni; Kathleen Keller; Huntley Funsten; and Elise Bauman. We are grateful to you all.

> *Jean Withrow*
> *Gay Brookes*
> *Martha Clark Cummings*

Preface: To the Student

In *Changes*, you will do a lot of reading, and you will write a lot about what you have read. Sometimes it will seem like you have been writing forever, and you will turn the page and find that the next section of the chapter you are working on is called "Topics for Writing." There is a reason for this.

Changes is a book designed to help you see and work with connections between your ideas and the ideas of other writers. In the book you will be asked to read, to pay attention to what you feel and think as you are reading, and to write about your thoughts and feelings. Your understanding of and responses to others' writing, including that of your classmates, will become the basis of your own writing.

As you read this book, you will be writing your own "book," your *reading log* or reading journal, which can be a spiral or loose-leaf notebook. In it, you will write your thoughts about and reactions to what you read. When you look back at these thoughts and reactions, you will easily find ideas for your written pieces on related topics. We ask you to do this because this is what professional writers do. They spend a great deal of time reading, thinking, and writing down their ideas before they actually start writing a story or an essay or a poem.

One set of activities, Before Reading, After Reading, and Topics for Writing, asks you to write as a way of making connections. The Before Reading activities ask you to bring to mind what you already know about a topic. Once you have read the story or essay or poem, the After Reading activities ask you to respond to what you've read—to consider the text and to explore your feelings, thoughts, and interpretations—by writing in your log.

At this point, the writing you have done and the discussions you have had have prepared you for writing a more finished piece of your own. The activities in Topics for Writing offer you a choice of topics. But you are free to shape a topic to your own thinking in any way you want. This is the time to put your ideas in order, focus on a topic and the points you want to make, and come up with examples and reasons to "show" your thinking. The final section, After Writing, gives you a chance to share your ideas with a group and get feedback on your writing.

Another set of activities is designed to help you become aware of reading and writing processes. In How I Read It, you will look at your reading process in comparison to that of your classmates. In How It's Written, you'll do what accomplished writers do—that is, look at how a story, poem, or essay is written; in other words, you will read like writers. In After Writing, you will reflect on how you wrote. By becoming more aware of your own and others' reading and writing strategies, you'll become a stronger, more flexible reader and writer.

Many activities in this book suggest that you work with a group. You can learn a great deal by working with others, sharing ideas and interpretations, comparing reactions, and solving problems. Working in groups also gives you an opportunity to talk, and good talk leads to good thinking. When you engage in collaboration and conversation, your thinking changes, and you are enriched.

We hope the readings and activities in *Changes* will not only help you develop as readers, writers, and thinkers in English, but will also give you new ways of thinking about *change*.

Contents

Chapter 3
Birth/Death   77

Chapter 5
Change and Resisting Change   163

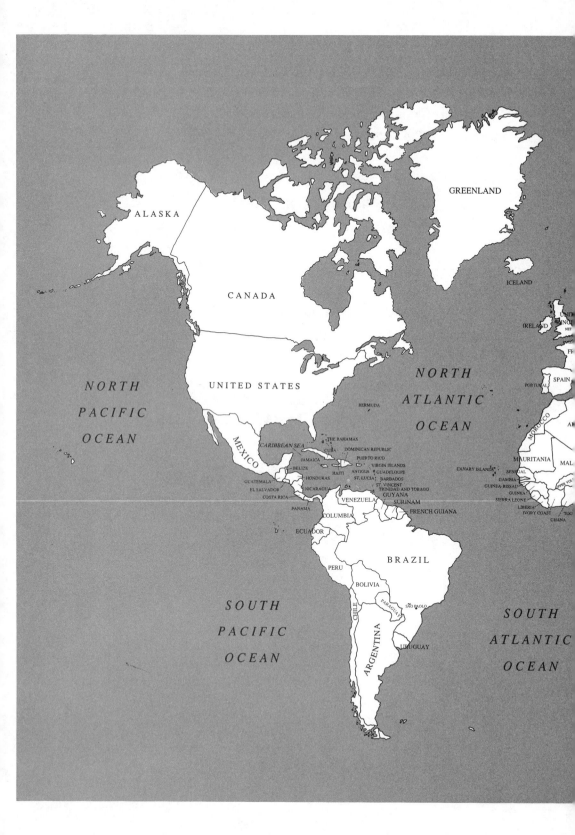

FINLAND

SOVIET UNION

POLAND

CZECH...
HUNGARY
...GOSLAVIA BULGARIA
ROMANIA
GREECE   TURKEY

NISIA

LIBYA   EGYPT

CHAD   SUDAN

CENT. AFR. REPUB.

ON...   ETHIOPIA
CONGO   ZAIRE   UGANDA
                 KENYA
         BURUNDI RWANDA
         TANZANIA

ANGOLA
      ZAMBIA
      ZIMBABWE MOZAMBIQUE
NAMIBIA BOTSWANA   MALAWI
                           MADAGASCAR
SOUTH   SWAZILAND
AFRICA   LESOTHO
         TRANSKEI

SYRIA
LEBAN... IRAQ   IRAN
ISRAEL
JORDAN
      KUWAIT
SAUDI   QATAR
ARABIA   U. ARAB EMIRATES
              OMAN
YEMEN YEMEN (N)
DJIBOUTI

SOMALIA

MONGOLIA

PEOPLE'S REPUBLIC OF CHINA

AFGHANISTAN
         PAKISTAN
              NEPAL   BHUTAN
         INDIA   BURMA
              BANGLADESH
                   LAO...
              THAILAND
SRI LANKA   VIETNAM
                  KAMPUCHEA
         SINGAPORE   MALAYSIA
                  SUMATRA
                     INDONESIA

N. KOREA
S. KOREA   JAPAN

TAIWAN

HONG KONG

PHILIPPINES

PACIFIC

OCEAN

PAPUA NEW
GUINEA

SOLOMON ISLANDS

AUSTRALIA

INDIAN   OCEAN

NEW ZEALAND

Changes

Readings for ESL Writers

Chapter 1

Leaving/Arriving

1. The title of this chapter is "Leaving/Arriving."

   a. In your reading log, **freewrite** for 5 minutes whatever comes to your mind about the word *leaving*. (See Appendix A.1, p. 201, for an explanation and examples of freewriting.)
   b. Reread what you wrote.
   c. Write one sentence that summarizes the most important thing you said (the **kernel** idea). (See Appendix A.1., p. 201.)
   d. Do the same thing for the word *arriving*.

2. Form a group with three other students. Read your two sentences to your group. Talk about what is alike and what is different in what you and your group members wrote.

3. What connections do you see between what you wrote in your log and the title of this book, *Changes*?
   Talk about the connections with your group and then with the class.

BEFORE READING

1. Look at the title of this story. With your class, make a **cluster** of the words you associate with this title. (See Appendix A.2, pp. 204–206, for an explanation and examples of clustering.)

2. Now read the story.

Leaving Home Behind
Melba Cruz

Melba Cruz was a student at Borough of Manhattan Community College in New York City when she wrote this composition. It appeared in a student publication called ESL Voices.

Eighteen years ago I had in my hands an airplane ticket which allowed me to leave my country and come to the U.S.A. For many people it could be the realization of their dream. For me it was frustration and pain. I planned to leave the house early in the morning because I had the sensation that the good-byes of my little kids would be the same as, "You are running away from us." I was afraid to see their innocent faces and hear their voices saying, "See you some day." But they were more astute than I was. That day they awoke earlier than usual. They wanted to see my departure. Before I was up, they were dressed up and sitting in the front door of the house.

They kissed me and hugged me and said good-bye. But that day is still in my heart and mind. I remember their faces, their smiles, and the pair of small hands waving at a car which was moving away very fast.

AFTER READING

1. In your reading log, write answers to these questions:

   What do you understand or see in what you just read?

   How do you feel about what you understand or see?

What do you associate with your understanding? (See Appendix B.1, p. 209, for an explanation and examples.)

Share your writing with your group.

2. Choose one person's writing to read to the class.

HOW I READ IT

How did clustering words around the title help you prepare for reading this story? Write for a few minutes in your reading log. Share your writing with the class.

TOPICS FOR WRITING

Choose one activity.

Activity A: Write about an experience you had leaving a place. In one or two paragraphs tell what happened, how you felt, and what you especially remember about it.

Activity B: Write a composition (a story, a poem, an essay) with the title "Leaving Home Behind."

AFTER WRITING

Read your composition to your group. As a group, tell what you like about each composition. Then choose one composition to read to the class.

BEFORE READING

1. Read the introductory information on these two stories. Then, with a partner, locate the People's Republic of China and Haiti on a map.

2. Pick *one* of the stories and read it.

Freedom/At Sea
Iu-choi Chan/Bernardin Monestime

These two stories were written by students who eventually escaped from their countries and came to the United States. "Freedom" is Iu-choi Chan's story of his first attempt to leave the People's Republic of China. He wrote the story while he was a student at California State University in Bakersfield. "At Sea" is Bernardin Monestime's story of his first try at escaping from Haiti. He wrote his story while he was a student at Borough of Manhattan Community College in New York City.

FREEDOM

Two years ago, I attempted to escape from mainland China to Hong Kong. I planned and prepared well. I dressed up like a farmer and walked for two days from my village to the border between China and Hong Kong. That night, I was very excited and nervous, but I tried to keep calm. At the border there were a lot of sentries who tried to catch people like me, so I put some mud on myself to avoid being noticed. It was not easy for me to pass through the sentries, but I bit my tongue and climbed across the swampy area. Finally, I reached the river that runs across the border. I plunged into it. It was icy cold, and I used all my strength to swim as fast as I could. In about twenty minutes, I touched land. I had made it! My happiness was beyond description. But when I stood up, a Hong Kong policeman was immediately beside me. My dream was shattered. I was taken to a police station to wait for a truck that takes unsuccessful refugees back to China. The police put me in the truck with a great many other people, and we were driven like a herd of buffalo back to China. I had lost my freedom again.

AT SEA

I came from a small island in Haiti. The population is about 20,000. Most of us are family. This island is the richest island in Haiti. Most of us work on farms, make boats, or fish. Our favorite food is fish, plantains, potatoes, and rice, and of course we drink the milk of coconuts.

In 1978 a group of us decided to leave the island for a different life. We thought Miami, Florida, would be our new homeland because it was near the sea. We decided to leave the island on July 23, 1978. After reading the map, we decided it would take us 10 days to get to Florida.

After two days on the voyage, a big wind rose and sank our boat. Now all of us were in the sea. We didn't know what to do, where to go, or where we were at. We were lost. We didn't know where north or west was. We were all good swimmers, but it was too far to go back to the island. I thought all of us were going to be killed by some big fish, but I continued swimming anyway. After three hours of swimming, one of our group got lost. We couldn't see where he was because it was night. We spent 15 minutes looking for him, but we couldn't find him. I thought maybe he was eaten by a fish. We continued swimming. Finally, after about 20 minutes, we heard a motorboat. We yelled for help, and the boat came close to us and picked us up. It was a Dominican boat. Now we wanted to tell them about the missing person, but none of us could speak Spanish. We tried to tell them with sign language and they eventually understood us. Now they searched for the missing one. After 25 minutes they found him dead. A fish had eaten his right leg. We pulled him on board and covered his body, and the boat took us back to the island.

A year later we tried again, and this time we made it to Miami, Florida. This is a true story of my life.

AFTER READING

1. Make a **double entry** in your reading log: On the left page of your notebook, write a short summary of the story. (That is, tell what happened in no more than two sentences.) On the right page, write your response: reactions, feelings, thoughts, questions, and so on. (See Appendix B.2, pp. 211–13, for an explanation and examples of double entries.) Share your writing with your group.

2. In your group, pick one summary of each story and one response to read to the class. As a class, talk about similarities and differences in what people wrote.

HOW I READ IT

1. Quickly make a list of some of the words you remember from the story you read. Then reread the story looking for two or three words to add to your list. (They can be new words, words you like and want to remember, or words to use in your own writing.)

2. *How* did you read when you reread? What did you do differently from the first time you read the story? For example, did you read more slowly or more quickly? Did you skip parts, or did you read every word? What did you do when you came to a word you didn't understand? Write answers to these questions in your reading log for a few minutes. Then share your writing with your group.

3. As a class, make a list of some of the **reading strategies** (techniques) people used when reading the story the first and second times.

    What did you learn about *reading* from this activity? How could this help you in the future? Talk about these questions with the class. (See Appendix C, p. 219, for more explanation and examples.)

TOPICS FOR WRITING

Work with a partner. Choose one activity.

Activity A: With your partner, retell "Freedom" or "At Sea" from the point of view of the Hong Kong policeman who caught Iu-choi Chan or one of the Dominicans who rescued Bernardin Monestime. It may help to make a **list** of the events and details in the order in which they happened. Then each person writes the story. Include enough details for a reader to see exactly what happened.

Activity B: Imagine that you are reporters for your school or town newspaper. You are going to write a news report of the story you read. Together, *list* the important facts and details in the order in which you want to tell them. You will probably want to include answers to the questions *who, what, where, when, how,* and *why.*

    Then each person writes the news report with a suitable headline. (You may first want to analyze a news report from a newspaper. What kind of information is given in the headline? In the first paragraph? In the rest of the story?)

Activity C: Both Chan and Monestime were unsuccessful in their attempts to leave their countries. Think of an unsuccessful escape (your own or that of someone you know). First, tell your partner your story from beginning to end, including enough details for your listener to understand exactly what happened. It may help you to make a **list** of the events and details in the order in which they happened. Then each person writes the story. (See Appendix A.3, p. 204, for an explanation and examples of making lists.)

AFTER WRITING

1. Form a group with others who did the same activity as you did. Read your story to your group. Ask your listeners to retell what they understood.

2. Write in your log about **how you wrote** this composition. For example, what did you do first? Next? How many times did you write it? Did you change anything? (See Appendix D, p. 220, for more explanation.)

BEFORE READING

1. Read the introductory information. Given this information, write down one question you expect the story to answer for you. Read your question to your group. Make a list of the questions, and share them with the class.
2. With the class, locate Antigua and England on the map following p. xix.
3. Listen to your instructor read the first paragraph of the story. Write down quickly what facts you know about the story so far. Share these with the class.
4. Read the rest of the story silently.

A Walk to the Jetty
Jamaica Kincaid

The novel Annie John *by Jamaica Kincaid tells of one girl's growing into adolescence on the Caribbean island of Antigua. At the end of the novel, we see Annie at the age of 17 leaving her parents and her home to study nursing in England. "A Walk to the Jetty" is the title of the last chapter of the novel.*

"My name is Annie John." These were the first words that came into my mind as I woke up on the morning of the last day I spent in Antigua, and they stayed there, lined up one behind the other, marching up and down, for I don't know how long. At noon on that day, a ship on which I was to be a passenger would sail to Barbados, and there I would board another ship, which would sail to England, where I would study to become a nurse. My name was the last thing I saw the night before, just as I was falling asleep; it was written in big, black letters all over my trunk, sometimes followed by my address in Antigua, sometimes followed by my address as it would be in England. I did not want to go to England, I did not want to be a nurse, but I would have chosen going off to live in a cavern and keeping house for seven unruly men rather than go on with my life as it stood. I never wanted to lie in this bed again, my legs hanging out way past the foot of it, tossing and turning on my mattress, with its cotton stuffing all lumped just where it wasn't a good place to be lumped. I never wanted to lie in my bed again and hear Mr. Ephraim driving his sheep to pasture—a signal to my mother that she should get up to prepare my father's and my bath and breakfast. I never wanted to lie in my bed and hear her get dressed, washing her face, brushing her teeth, and gargling. I especially never wanted to lie in my bed and hear my mother gargling again.

Lying there in the half-dark of my room, I could see my shelf, with my books—some of them prizes I had won in school, some of them gifts from my mother—and with photographs of people I was supposed to love forever no matter what, and with my old thermos, which was given to me for my eighth birthday, and some shells I had gathered at different times I spent at the sea. In one corner stood my washstand and its beautiful basin of white enamel with blooming red hibiscus painted at the bottom and an urn that matched. In another corner were my old school shoes and my Sunday shoes. In still another corner, a bureau held my old clothes. I knew everything in this room, inside out and outside in. I had lived in this room for thirteen of my seventeen years. I could see in my mind's eye even the day my father was adding it onto the rest of the house. Everywhere I looked stood something that had meant a lot to me, that had given me pleasure at some point, or could remind me of a time that was a happy time. But as I was lying there my heart could have burst open with joy at the thought of never having to see any of it again.

If someone had asked me for a little summing up of my life at that moment as I lay in bed, I would have said, "My name is Annie John. I was born on the fifteenth of September, seventeen years ago, at Holberton Hospital, at five o'clock in the morning. At the time I was born, the moon was going down at one end of the sky and the sun was coming up at the other. My mother's name is Annie also. My father's name is Alexander, and he is thirty-five years older than my mother. . . . The house we live in my father built with his own hands. The bed I am lying in my father built with his own hands. If I get up and sit on a chair, it is a chair my father built with his own hands. When my mother uses a large wooden spoon to stir the porridge we sometimes eat as part of our breakfast, it will be a spoon that my father has carved with his own hands. The sheets on my bed my mother made with her own hands. The curtains hanging at my window my mother made with her own hands. The nightie I am wearing, with scalloped neck and hem and sleeves, my mother made with her own hands. When I look at things in a certain way, I suppose I should say that the two of them made me with their own hands. For most of my life, when the three of us went anywhere together I stood between the two of them or sat between the two of them. But then I got too big, and there I was, shoulder to shoulder with them more or less, and it became not very comfortable to walk down the street together. And so now there they are together and here I am apart. I don't see them now the way I used to, and I don't love them now the way I used to. The bitter thing about it is that they are just the same and it is I who have changed, so all the things I used to be and all the things I used to feel are as false as the teeth in my father's head. . . ."

Lying in my bed for the last time, I thought, This is what I add up to. At that, I felt as if someone had placed me in a hole and was forcing me first down and then up against the pressure of gravity. I shook myself and prepared to get up. I said to myself, "I am getting up out of this bed for the last time." Everything I would do that morning until I got on the ship that would take me to England I would be doing for the last time, for I had made up my mind that, come what may, the road for me now went only in one direction: away from my home, away from my mother, away from my father, away from the everlasting blue sky, away from the everlasting hot sun, away from people who said to me, "This happened during the time your mother was carrying you." If I had been asked to put into words why I felt this way, if I had been given years to reflect and come up with the words of why I felt this way, I would not have been able to come up with so much as the letter "A." I only knew that I felt the way I did, and that this feeling was the strongest thing in my life. . . .

Now . . . I had nothing to take my mind off what was happening to me. My mother and my father—I was leaving them forever. My home on an island—I was leaving it forever. What to make of everything? I felt a familiar hollow space inside. I felt I was being held down against my will. I felt I was burning up from head to toe. I felt that someone was tearing me up into little pieces and soon I would be able to see all the little pieces as they floated out into nothing in the deep blue sea. I didn't know whether to laugh or cry. I could see that it would be better not to think too clearly about any one thing. The launch was being made ready to take me, along with some other passengers, out to the ship that was anchored in the sea. My father paid our fares, and we joined a line of people waiting to board. My mother checked my bag to make sure that I had my passport, the money she had given me, and a sheet of paper placed between some pages in my Bible on which were written the names of the relatives—people I had not known existed—with whom I would live in England. Across from the jetty was a wharf, and some stevedores were loading and unloading barges. I don't know why seeing that struck me so, but suddenly a wave of strong feeling came over me, and my heart swelled with a great gladness as the words "I shall never see this again" spilled out inside me. But then, just as quickly, my heart shriveled up and the words "I shall never see this again" stabbed at me. I don't know what stopped me from falling in a heap at my parents' feet.

When we were all on board, the launch headed out to sea. Away from the jetty, the water became the customary blue, and the launch left a wide path in it that looked like a road. I passed by sounds and smells that were so familiar that I had long ago stopped paying any attention to them. But now here they were, and the ever-present "I shall never see this again" bobbed up and down inside me. There was the sound of the seagull diving down into the water and coming up with something silverish in its mouth. There was the smell of the sea and the sight of small pieces of rubbish floating around in it. There were boats filled with fishermen coming in early. There was the sound of their voices as they shouted greetings to each other. There was the hot sun, there was the blue sea, there was the blue sky. Not very far away, there was the white sand of the shore, with the run-down houses all crowded in next to each other, for in some places only poor people lived near the shore. I was seated in the launch between my parents, and when I realized that I was gripping their hands tightly I glanced quickly to see if they were looking at me with scorn, for I felt sure that they must have known of my never-see-this-again feelings. But instead my father kissed me on the forehead and my mother kissed me on the mouth, and they both gave over their hands to me, so that I could grip them as much as I wanted. I was on the verge of feeling that it had all been a mistake, but I remembered that I wasn't a child anymore, and that now when I made up my mind about something I had to see it through. At that moment, we came to the ship, and that was that.

The goodbyes had to be quick, the captain said. My mother introduced herself to him and then introduced me. She told him to keep an eye on me, for I had never gone this far away from home on my own. She gave him a letter to pass on to the captain of the next ship that I would board in Barbados. They walked me to my cabin, a small space that I would share with someone else—a woman I did not know. I had never before slept in a room with someone I did not know. My father kissed me goodbye and told me to be good and to write home often. After he said this, he looked at me, then looked at the floor and swung his left foot, then looked at me again. I could see that he wanted to say something else, something that he had never said to me before, but then he just turned and walked away. My mother said, "Well," and then she threw her arms around me. Big tears streamed down her face, and it must have been that—for I could not bear to see my mother cry—which started me crying, too. She then tightened her arms around me and held me to her close, so that I felt that I couldn't breathe. With that, my tears dried up and I was suddenly on my guard. "What does she want now?" I said to myself. Still holding me close to her, she said, in a voice that raked across my skin, "It doesn't matter what you do or where you go, I'll always be your mother and this will always be your home."

I dragged myself away from her and backed off a little, and then I shook myself, as if to wake myself out of a stupor. We looked at each other for a long time with smiles on our faces, but I know the opposite of that was in my heart. As if responding to some invisible cue, we both said, at the very same moment, "Well." Then my mother turned around and walked out the cabin door. I stood there for I don't know how long, and then I remembered that it was customary to stand on deck and wave to your relatives who were returning to shore. From the deck, I could not see my father, but I could see my mother facing the ship, her eyes searching to pick me out. I removed from my bag a red cotton handkerchief that she had earlier given me for this purpose, and I waved it wildly in the air. Recognizing me immediately, she waved back just as wildly, and we continued to do this until she became just a dot in the matchbox-size launch swallowed up in the big blue sea.

I went back to my cabin and lay down on my berth. Everything trembled as if it had a spring at its very center. I could hear the small waves lap-lapping around the ship. They made an unexpected sound, as if a vessel filled with liquid had been placed on its side and now was slowly emptying out.

AFTER READING

1. Write an answer in your reading log to one or two of the questions you or your classmates asked before reading the story. Share your answers with the class.

2. In your reading log, make a **double entry**: On the left page of your notebook, copy sentences, phrases, or ideas that interest you, or tell in your own words some of what you understood. On the right page of your notebook, write your reactions, feelings, thoughts, associations, and so on. (See Appendix B.2, pp. 211–13, for an explanation and examples of double entries.) Reread the story as necessary.

   Share your writing with your group.

3. Choose one activity.

   Activity A: On pages 10 and 11, Annie mentioned several times the words "I shall never see this again" and referred to her "never-see-this-again feelings." Reread these pages. Explain in writing how this thought made her feel. How do you know? Read your writing to your group.

   Activity B: Imagine that you are a reporter from the school newspaper interviewing Annie as to why she felt so strongly about getting away. First, reread the passage for ideas, especially pp. 8–10; then write the interview (both your questions and Annie's answers). Read your writing to your group.

HOW I READ IT

1. How did asking questions before reading affect how you read the story? What purpose do you see in asking questions *before* reading something? With the class, talk about the use of questions before reading.

2. Reread the text, and circle five words you don't understand. Share your words with your group. As a group, try to figure out the meaning of each person's circled words by looking at the contexts in which the words appear or by consulting with each other. When absolutely necessary, use a dictionary.

3. How can you get clues to the meanings of words from context? Talk about this with the class.

   Write a few sentences in your reading log about this reading strategy.

HOW IT'S WRITTEN

1. Work with another person. Choose one activity.

   Activity A: Reread the piece, looking for words and phrases Kincaid used to describe *colors* and *sounds*. Circle these.

   Activity B: Reread the piece, looking for figures of speech that show comparison, such as similes and metaphors, used to describe feelings and events. Underline these.

   Note: A *simile* is a comparison of two unlike things usually using the words *like* or *as*.

   EXAMPLES:

   (1) "The launch left a wide path in it that looked *like* a road."

   (2) "They made an unexpected sound, *as if* a vessel filled with liquid had been placed on its side and now was slowly emptying out."

   Note: A *metaphor* uses a term that ordinarily stands for one thing to stand for another; it thus implies that one thing *is* another.

   EXAMPLES:

   (1) "The words 'I shall never see this again' stabbed at me." (This implies that words are a knife, capable of stabbing.)

(2) "a voice that raked across my skin" (This implies that a voice is a rake.)

2. Share your findings with your group.

3. Talk about this with the class: How did Kincaid help the reader understand the story and Annie's feelings by using these kinds of details and images?

4. Write in your log about what you learned about writing from these activities.

TOPICS FOR WRITING

Choose one activity.

Activity A: Annie John left her parents and her country behind. Make a list of kinds of leaving you have experienced. Choose one experience, and write one or two paragraphs about what happened, how you felt, and why the event was significant. Think about the colors you saw and the sounds you heard (loud or soft, pleasant or unpleasant). Try to include details of sound and color or figures of speech that show comparison.

Activity B: Write about an experience this story reminds you of. Tell what happened, how you felt, and why the event was significant. Do you remember the color of people's clothes or the colors of any objects in the setting? What sounds do you remember hearing? Try to include details of sound and color or figures of speech that show comparison.

Activity C: Bernardin Monestime said he left Haiti for a different life. Make a list of reasons people leave one country for another. Put your list into categories and give a title to each category (for example, "Political"). Then interview some of your classmates to find out why they left their country (if they did). Put them, along with Monestime, Iu-choi Chan, and Annie John, into the appropriate categories. Finally, write a composition about why people leave one country for another, using your own experience and the experiences of these people as examples.

(*Note*: You may want to try a technique called **cubing** to help you gather ideas. See Appendix A.4, p. 208, for an explanation of cubing.)

AFTER WRITING

1. Read your writing to your group. Ask your listeners to restate what they understood your important point to be and to tell what details especially stand out for them.

2. Give your story a title, if you haven't already done so.

3. Write in your log about how you wrote this composition. For example, was it easy or difficult to think of sounds, colors, and figures of speech? Did you use any special technique to gather ideas?

BEFORE READING

1. Read the introductory information.

2. Look at the title of the passage. With your class, make a *cluster* of words you associate with the title. Talk about what the title means.

3. Look through the passage. Notice a small break (marked by *). As you're reading, when you get to this break, write in your reading log one thing that is in your mind (for example, a question, reaction, confusion, thought, image). Do the same when you come to the end of the story.

Now read "To the Melting Pot."

To the Melting Pot
Liu Zongren

Liu Zongren, a journalist from the People's Republic of China, spent two years in the United States as an exchange scholar studying journalism and English. His book, Two Years in the Melting Pot, *is a record of his experiences and observations while in the United States. The excerpt below describes Liu's departure from China and his arrival in Washington, D.C.*

It was a cold, late-November day in 1980. I had allowed only my wife, Fengyun, and my son, Ze, to bring me to the airport and see me off. I was about to leave Beijing, China, to study in the United States on a two-year fellowship. In a country that has very little currency to spend on scholars traveling abroad, I was fortunate to be one of the very few selected.

We arrived promptly at 11:00 P.M., and after checking in we found that many of the forty-six visiting scholars, bound for many different U.S. universities, were already there. Fengyun looked sad and my heart ached. I wanted to take her in my arms and tell her how much I would miss her, but that is not the Chinese custom. She is a strong-willed person who had been keeping her emotions in check for a long time, but today I saw her eyes shimmering. Although we really hadn't said much to each other in the past several days, we now seemed to have exhausted all words. What could I say to her? She fussed with my travel bag and scolded me: "Don't lose your things—you always forget something. The woolen underwear is at the bottom of your case. Put it on when you get there. They say Chicago is very cold."

For the past half month I had been so wrapped up in my own problems and preparations that, in the last days, she complained about my neglecting her—I should not have squeezed onto the bus the way I did the other day; I should have given her more love and comfort. Now I wanted to apologize and tell her I understood. I looked at her face. She was thirty-four this year, a beautiful woman I had known for fifteen years. Now her skin was not so smooth anymore. How time flies. And in all of those years, with all that had happened, how few happy periods we had had together. Now we were to be separated, again. . . .

I turned to my wife. "Take care of yourself, Fengyun. We'll make up for our loss when I come home."

I hurried to catch up with the others. When I turned to look back, I saw Fengyun weeping. Even when I was taken away in 1973 for a two year stay in a labor reformation center, during the Cultural Revolution, she hadn't shed a tear.

As I walked toward the plane I wondered if this journey would be worth the sacrifice to my personal life. When I had confessed to friends that I was not enthusiastic about going away, some didn't believe me. They thought I was pretending to be modest, and Fengyun warned me not to say such silly things. It was a paradox. On the one hand, I had been eager to win this chance, which would give me two years to look at a foreign country and would enhance my reputation. I often felt that others in the office of *China Reconstructs*, where I worked as an English translator, looked down on my abilities because I had never gone to college. This would rectify that situation. But on the other hand, I hated to leave my family, as I had been forced to do just a few years before. By nature I was a homebody; I disliked traveling, even inside China. For these others, who were walking now beside me onto the plane, study abroad might be a joy, a free vacation trip. For me, it would only be an opportunity to improve my professional skills. . . .

It was midday and I was tired from this long journey as we began the final part of our flight, across the Atlantic Ocean, to land at Washington, D.C. How would I be treated in America? How would I feel being alone there? At the orientation, a Chinese diplomat briefed us on how to behave at a dinner table, how to use silverware and how to dress. A vice-minister encouraged us to study hard for the cause of building socialist China and for the country's modernization. I am basically a proud person and a conservative Chinese. I have a tendency to keep my distance from certain colleagues I don't like. I was disturbed by the idea that I might be expected to respond humbly to others. In the U.S. I would have to relate to

Americans, whether I like it or not, and Americans sometimes can be arrogant and aloof.

Yet, there I was, about to realize one of my greatest ambitions, to study and live in America. But where was the elation I should be feeling?

I remembered a line from a poem I once wrote about my youth: "My thoughts fly above the clouds. My ambition rides with the wind."

*

After a flight of twenty-two hours, we crossed over the coast of the United States and prepared for our landing at Dulles International Airport in Virginia, twenty miles west of Washington, D.C. . . .

While the other members of our group stayed busy, taking tours and exploring the beautiful capital of the richest country in the world, I stayed alone, feeling sad and dislodged. I was suffering from jetlag and nostalgia, missing Fengyun and Ze. It was during these days that I wrote Fengyun my first letter from America:

> The temperature is much the same here as in Beijing. The difference is that everywhere there is green grass. There are no crowds of people on the street. The stores are quiet and empty most of the time. I don't know how they make a living selling so little.
>
> Our son would like this place; there are squirrels everywhere! Flocks of pigeons are fed in open lots and on sidewalks. You don't feel squeezed in as we do on Beijing streets. There is so much space. Most museums are free and in them are hundreds of TV sets showing educational programs. In the windows of stores, TVs are on all day and night. Nobody bothers to turn off the lights even during the day.
>
> Cars and more cars—as many cars as we have bicycles. Very few people walk. There are also very few public buses. Most people drive cars, even old women drive.
>
> At the embassy kitchen we have chicken every meal. We could have a whole chicken if we could eat it. We have apples, oranges and bananas at every meal, plenty of them. Plenty of milk. They say Americans drink milk like we drink water. But I have little appetite. This may be caused by jetlag, but I think the real reason is that I don't feel comfortable here.

During my two years in the United States, I would often wonder why I had been willing to leave Fengyun. Although it isn't unusual in modern-day China for families to be separated for long periods of time, I would continue to be amazed that I had made such a choice.

AFTER READING

1. Choose one activity.

   Activity A: *Freewrite* for 10 minutes about what you have just read.

   Activity B: Write answers to these three questions:
   What do you understand or see in what you read?
   How do you feel about what you understand or see?
   What do you associate with your understanding? (See Appendix B.1, pp. 209–210, for an explanation and examples.)

   Share your reading log with your group.

2. As a group, write a couple of questions you'd like to ask the author, Liu Zongren. Reread the passage as needed.

3. Discuss your questions with the class. See if you can answer any of them.

HOW I READ IT

1. Think about how you read this passage the first time. What did you do when you came to a word, a phrase, or a sentence you didn't understand? Recall a specific instance, and write down what you did.

2. Find out what others in your group did when they did not understand. Make a list of strategies. Share your list with the class.

3. In your log, describe a new strategy (one you just learned about) that you can use when reading something you don't understand. (See Appendix C, p. 219, for an explanation and examples.)

TOPICS FOR WRITING

Choose one activity.

Activity A: Liu refers to the United States as a "melting pot." What does the expression "melting pot" mean to you? Explain in writing. Use examples from your own experience or the experience of others to illustrate your ideas.

Activity B: Write a letter to Liu Zongren responding to this passage from his book and asking him some of the questions you still have about his experience in the United States. (You can write him in care of the publisher of his book, China Books and Periodicals, Inc., San Francisco, CA.)

Activity C: In her introduction to Liu's book, Linda Yu, a reporter for WLL-TV in Chicago, says that the United States has long been a melting pot but that because it has accepted so many people, ideas, languages, and customs, many Americans do not welcome more. Do you agree or disagree with her idea that many Americans do not welcome new people, ideas, and so on? Explain in writing. Use your own experience or the experience of others to illustrate your ideas.

Note: As a way of collecting and focusing ideas before writing, you may want to do one of the following:

1. *Freewrite* on the topic for 10 minutes; write a *kernel* sentence; freewrite on the kernel sentence; write another kernel sentence (**looping**). (See Appendix A.2, pp. 201–204, for an explanation.)
2. Make a **cluster** of words and ideas on the topic.
3. Make one or more **lists** of words and ideas on the topic.
4. Do some **cubing** on the topic. (See Appendix A, p. 208, for explanation.)

AFTER WRITING

1. Put your writing away for a day or two. Then reread it *as though you were a reader*. Respond in writing, answering these questions. (See Appendix E, p. 222, for an explanation and examples.)
   a. What point does this piece make? Is it clear?
   b. What do I like about this writing?
2. Share your writing with your group.

BEFORE READING
---

1. Read the introductory information and title.

2. What do you think the title means? Talk about the title with the class. (*Note:* Your class may want to read lines 15 and 16 of the poem on p. 34. The title "Worlds to Go Before I Sleep" is based on these lines.)

3. With a partner, locate Cambodia on the map.

4. Look through the passage. Note the small breaks (marked by *). While reading, when you get to each break, stop and write down in your reading log one thing that is in your mind (for example, a question, reaction, confusion, association, thought, image, or prediction). Now read "Worlds to Go Before I Sleep."

Worlds to Go Before I Sleep
Gail Sheehy

Gail Sheehy, an American writer, met the Cambodian girl Phat Mohm in a refugee camp in Thailand and later arranged for Mohm to enter the United States as her foster child. In this chapter from Sheehy's book about Mohm, Spirit of Survival, *the girl and the author alternate in telling the story of Mohm's arrival in New York City.*

When I step onto the airplane, I feel good. That's it—I passed everything!

I never fly before, never travel to another country. I don't know there is anyplace else. I know there's Thailand, but you could walk to it. We sit in the back of the airplane, all fifteen minors. One other girl, Suon Unn, sits next to me. The fly lady stands up front and waves her arms around. And then the back of the airplane drops down and—ooohh—my stomach!

Children all around me start throwing up.

Stand up, walk around, relax, think about what makes me happy . . . a lily pond in Cambodia . . . to take my mind out.

Quick try to find my monkey balm, rub it on.

They take us off the plane to sleep for a while and then they take us on another airplane. This time the fly ladies all have white faces, must be American.

"What is it?" Unn holds up the bag of food.

"Don't ask me. I live in the city, but I never see that before."

I try it. Hard, salty. The fly lady says, "Peanut." She gives me a cup: "Coke, good, try it!" It's more sweet than a sugarcane stick. I guess this is American dinner.

They bring a tray with sticky yellow stuff and gooey white stuff and dark brown stuff—no fruit or vegetable, nothing I ever see before. Unn is very sick. I show her how to put her head in the little sick bag.

Look out the window. I see the sun rise and after a few hours, the sun set—up, down, day and night passing so fast—time is speeding. I keep wondering, "Where does the sky end?" because I know the world is flat.

Unn's little sister has to go to the bathroom. She asks me to guard the door for her. So long she stays in there, the plane is bumping, the fly lady wants me to sit down. "Come out!" I call. She doesn't come. I sit down and after a while I forget about her. Suddenly I hear her, she's screaming. She's locked inside. She can't get out! I stand outside the door and tell her what to do—don't ask me how I know. Finally she opens it a crack. Poor girl. She is standing up on top of the seat and trying to pour water down the hole from a paper cup. That's how the bathroom works in Cambodia. But it's different here. It's too disgusting to tell her about.

The plane stops somewhere [in Seattle]. They call my name first, and all the children have to get off. Some go this way, some that, suddenly all my friends are gone. "I'm Customs," the man says. "Have to look inside your bag and check your identification." I show inside my plastic bag. I want to show my letter from the newspaper lady but he doesn't want it. I have the feeling it's going to be important at some point. It's like a ticket—to show somebody wants me.

A woman leads us to the next airplane, three of us left. Unn, myself, and a boy. What happened to all the others? It's so sad. I don't know where I am, how long we have to go or how short.

Only a few hours I sleep but when I wake up the sun rose again. Time speeding past. "Oh, my God," I think, "now I'm in a different world!"

The fly lady makes an announcement, I don't know what, but then I hear the words—*New York*—what beautiful words! That's the world I'm supposed to go to. But I don't know if anybody is going to be there.

*

At 9:42 P.M., E. S. T. a slip of a girl with hungry eyes and torn rubber sandals emerged from the flight canopy at Northwest Airlines. The world around me shrank to a soundless concentration. Our eyes met. A smile exploded in her face. I waved. She waved. Something wonderful stirred in my private regions of creation, and I felt tears of happiness flush down my face.

Our eyes bobbed between the thicknesses of other people until we reached each other. I embraced her and felt her meagerness. She looked up at me. Her eyes were immense, filled with light and hope, a child's eyes in a face no longer a child's.

As if from a great distance, I heard my sister saying, "She's beautiful, Gail."

*

Catholic Guardian Society had sent a bilingual social worker, Mr. Sao, who prompted me to try the few scraps I had of her language.

"*Chum riap sua.*" Hello. "*Nea' khlien bai te?*" Do you want to eat? No. "*Nea' chawng tau dek te?*" Do you want to sleep? No. "*Neh chawng tau bangkun te?*" Do you want to go to the bathroom? No. I asked if she was cold. Yes. Good. I had brought one of Maura's sweaters for her. I introduced my *bong srei*—"sister." Then I tried the phrase that means in Khmer "I love you."

"*Knhom sralanh nea'.*"

Her face whirled up at me, astonishment in it. Such an intimacy from a near stranger must have seemed very odd. But her face seemed to melt.

"I think you said the right thing," whispered Mr. Sao. He asked Mohm how she felt.

"*Sok sabai,*" she said, an expression that sounds exactly like what it means: calm, content, well in spirit.

She slipped her arm around my waist and we began to walk briskly into the bedlam of Kennedy Airport. Her long legs fell into synchrony with mine. It was a good sign. We were in step from the start.

*

I see her face, I know her face. She comes right to me and hugs me. That second I was so happy! But in the next second it was gone. I'm sure that happened to everybody.

What she says makes no sense to me. I never hear an accent before. Suddenly it's a different language, different people, some with faces white as cabbage, some with spots, some the color of soil—everything is different. Just pretend, "Oh well, it's normal."

She says, "I love you." It's funny to hear, it's wonderful. The man [Mr. Sao] tells me to call her "Mom." That's funny, too. Her name sounds like the way these people say my name. Mom. Is it the name for every woman here?

"Mom" drives her own car. She must be import[ant]. She has a sister who looks part Asia—she has short straight hair and her eyes are a little slanty—and she has a friend called General Chana; he can speak Khmer.

"Mom" tells him how I will live and he tells me. She has one daughter and two dogs, they live in the city but they have a porch over a park.

I think everybody in that car lives with her. But one by one they disappear. Just the two of us left. I cannot believe it. My idea was I would live with children from the camp. But no children. No one I know. Nothing I can speak. I don't know what it is, this big city. I don't [know] who she is—"Mom." I don't know what I'm going to turn out to be.

Sickening feeling . . . air so greasy, things fly around in the air you can't see, cars come together in a blind of light, screamy sirens, big trucks, buildings as tall as mountains fall over on us from both sides, oh no, I can't look. . . .

*

She was sick in the car. Of course. Travel by automobile was strange to her, as were most of the accouterments of urban life—elevators, intercoms, chains and locks and leashed dogs, not to mention shower taps and the magic instrument one holds to the ear and it talks back in a human voice.

At home, I showed her the terrace first. She seemed to like seeing all the trees across the street. I picked a flower for her. She picked a flower for me, copying my movements precisely. But I'd forgotten the rice! My sister went for takeout.

I showed her the room that would be hers, all to herself. She looked amazed. Gravitating to the picture of Maura, she must have grasped that this would be her sister, and she smiled. We turned on the light inside the new globe, and I traced her flight path from Bangkok to Tokyo to Seattle and across the United States. A frown rippled across her forehead. Then, recognition. She ventured her first English words. "New . . . New Yawk!"

She wanted to know about the two little animals who kept sniffing at her sandals. I gave her their names and we looked up the word *dog* in the dictionary. My sister returned with the container of Chinese rice, but Mohm looked at it as if at a well-meant mistake. I knew I had a lot to learn about marginal differences among Asian cultures, but rice—at least rice was a universal in the Orient, wasn't it?

"Show her the nightgown," my sister coached.

Mohm studied the granny gown, then pulled it over her fully clothed body. I coaxed off the sweater underneath and suggested she remove her jeans. She dipped her head modestly. I had to leave the room.

Maura telephoned from college. "Snuggle with her."

"I don't know, maybe she'd like to feel a little bit separate at first."

"Mom, she's only eight."

"I don't know what she is, her papers say fourteen."

"Oh, wow."

Suddenly I felt an arm slip around my waist from behind—Mohm. "I've gotta go, honey," I told Maura. "Call you tomorrow." Mohm was still fully clothed under the nightgown. Her body represented all the privacy she had; it would be fiercely guarded.

We took off the bedcovers together and I tucked her in. The dog jumped up and worked her rump into the crook of Mohm's waist. Would she like the dogs to sleep with her? I indicated. Her expression read as if I'd suggested she sleep in a tree. One thing I did know: Physical demonstrations of affection were severely inhibited in her culture. The head must not be touched; being the part of the body closest to God, it is sacred. And so, that first night, fully aware I was taking a chance but unable to restrain myself, I brushed her cheek with my lips.

"Goodnight, angel."

*

It's not what I expect, at all. I think America has log cabins with lots of land in between, I see a book about it. But this isn't even like Phnom Penh. Here the buildings have a thousand million little yellow windows, each one looks alike.

She show me the bathroom. It's as pretty as a house. I don't know how to push down the handle on the toilet, but I don't want to try anyway. We know from the letters minors send back how machines do everything in America. In American bathrooms you're supposed to sit on a seat and push a handle, and a hand comes out and cleans you! Disgusting!

She show me in the big word book the Khmer word *chkai*. She tell me it's the word for "dog." When I say the word after her, she clap her hands. Is that good? Is she angry?

A room alone, a bed alone. A dress to wear to bed. Where are my friends? Where is Unn? It's so different than Sakeo. We all sleep together there, seven or eight of us on little mats all in a row, together. If I close my eyes here, everything I know from before might fly away, I can never catch it again.

*

I poured myself a glass of wine and sat down to look through the plastic bag that represented the sum total of her worldly possessions. She had come with a tin spoon and the torn half of a file card stamped by the U.S. Immigration Service. Finding a certificate with her picture on it, pronouncing her a *theatre artiste* from Sakeo Holding Center Khmer Theatre, I smiled; this was a child who would not settle, no matter where she landed, for being a nobody. Underneath a parka issued by IRC [the International Rescue Committee] was a notebook in which she had been doing lessons, an elementary school book about the human body, and an envelope with three photographs—images of her housemother from Sakeo, Margie de Monchy, and Buddha. That was all she had, and she had abandoned it. On a dossier form provided by the UNHCR [United Nations High Commissioner for Refugees], the bare bones of her family history were recorded.

Zipped up inside a tiny red plastic pocketbook was a cloth, and inside the cloth, worn and folded and handled to a limp relic, I found the first letter from me. I wept.

What if I had been away on a trip? What if I hadn't listened to my messages? Her papers said nothing about a sponsor, my name was nowhere, the only address given was 80 Lafayette Street—the New York City Welfare Bureau. What if I hadn't shown up at the airport?

How was it possible that this child had come through genocide to a refugee camp and from there to an apartment on Fifth Avenue? Call it determination, call it luck; maybe it was destiny. But whatever help she may have had from fate, clearly this child had the soul of a survivor.

From her documents and possessions, it seemed virtually impossible to reconstruct the history of a survivor, from a family almost totally wiped out, from the wasteland of a country, from the habit of aliases and the patches of protective amnesia. I knew I would have to deal with her past eventually, but who was she *now*? What could I help her to become?

She was one of the first Cambodian refugees to be settled in New York State. And, among the thirteen co-sponsored by Catholic Guardian Society, she was the only girl. Plucky. I was infatuated with Mohm, but would I like her? Would she like me? Because the government did not yet permit one to adopt a refugee, she was officially a foster child, meaning that either of us could declare the "placement" hadn't worked out. But what was important now was not the rules of bureaucracy; it was the act of bonding, which we would have to do without a common language.

AFTER READING

1. Give your reading log to a partner. Read each other's responses to this passage. In your partner's log, write a short response to what your partner wrote. (*Note:* You may want to do How I Read It first and, after that, continue with After Reading 2.)

2. With your group, label each section of the story with the name of the person who was speaking (Mohm or Gail). Then, for each section, write down an important event detailed in that section. Share your work with the class.

3. Work with a partner.
   a. Reread the story, doing the following:

      One person: Put an X next to some things that were new, surprising, or strange to Mohm. In your log, make a list of these things, and beside each one, write some words that could describe how those things made her feel.

      The other person: Put an O next to some things that were new, surprising, or strange to Gail. In your log, make a list of these things, and beside each one, write some words that could describe how those things made her feel.

   b. Share your lists and words. Talk about this question: Did Mohm and Gail feel the same way or different?
   c. Find one way you think Mohm's and Gail's feelings were very different (or very much the same), and write for 5 minutes about this, connecting the feelings of Mohm and Gail in some way.
   d. Share your ideas with the class.

HOW I READ IT

1. Freewrite about *how* you read this passage the first time (about your *process* of reading). For example:

   Was it easy or difficult to read? Why?

   Did you reread anything? What? Why?

   What did you do when you didn't understand something?

2. Share your writing with the class.

   Did you learn any new reading strategies from hearing what other people said? If so, what?

   Are your reading strategies similar to other people's? Different?

   In your reading log write a response to these questions. (See Appendix C, p. 219, for more explanation and examples.)

HOW IT'S WRITTEN

1. With the class, talk about this: How did you decide who was speaking (Mohm or Gail)? What did Sheehy do to make the dif-

ferences clear to readers? Is Mohm's language different from Gail's? Explain.

2. Do you think Sheehy did a good job of showing when Mohm was speaking and when Gail was speaking?

TOPICS FOR WRITING

Choose one activity.

Activity A: Find the sentence on p. 25 where Mohm says, "It's not what I expect, at all." She was referring to the United States. Think about yourself when first coming to the United States or some other new place. What did you expect before you went, and what did you find when you got there? Were things what you expected they'd be? Explain in writing.

Activity B: Mohm had a number of thoughts and feelings during her plane trip and on her arrival in New York City. In what ways were these feelings similar to Liu Zongren's or to those of any person traveling to and arriving in a new place? How were they different? Explain in writing.

Activity C: Think of an experience you had in a new cultural setting where you didn't quite understand what was happening. Write it as a story, from beginning to end, including all the necessary details.

(*Note*: If you have trouble getting started, you may want to reread Appendix A, "Gathering Ideas," p. 201.)

AFTER WRITING

1. Exchange papers with a partner, and silently read each other's writing. After reading, write, on a separate piece of paper:
   a. One sentence restating the important point (as you understood it)
   b. One thing you especially like about the writing
   c. Any questions you have

2. Read each other's comments.

3. Write in your log about *how* you wrote this composition (your **process** of writing). Share your writing with your group. Talk about similarities and differences in writing strategies. (See Appendix D, p. 220, for more explanation of the writing process.)

BEFORE READING

1. Read the introductory information.

2. What words come to your mind when you see the title of this essay? Write them down in your log. Share them with the class.

3. Now read "Notes on Being a Foreigner."

Notes on Being a Foreigner
Alastair Reid

Alastair Reid is a travel writer for The New Yorker *magazine. He was born in Scotland, but he has lived most of his life in other lands, especially Spain, the United States, and Central America. He now owns a house in the Dominican Republic. Reid wrote "Notes on Being a Foreigner" in 1963 when he was in Geneva, Switzerland.*

I come suddenly into a foreign city, just as the lamps take light along the water, with some notes in my head. Arriving—the mood and excitement, at least, are always the same. I try out the language with the taxi driver, to see if it is still there; and later, I walk to a restaurant that is lurking round a corner in my memory. Nothing, of course, has changed; but cities flow on, like water, and, like water, they close behind any departure. We come back to confirm them, even though they do not particularly care. Or perhaps we come back to confirm ourselves?

*

Natives feel oddly toward foreigners. They may be hostile, aggressive, overfriendly, distant, or possessive; but at least they have the (to them) advantage of being in possession, so that between foreigners and themselves there is a moat with a drawbridge to which they keep the keys. Typical native gambits: "Why, we almost consider you one of us!" Or "What do you think of *our* (railways, king, public lavatories)?" Or "Are you familiar with our expression . . . ?" They have the assurance of Being In Possession.

*

And the foreigner? It depends on whether he is a foreigner by Necessity, Accident, or Choice. One thing, however, is sure: unless he regards being a foreigner as a positive state, he is doomed. If he has already chosen not to belong, then all the native gambits are bound to fail. But if he aspires to being a native, then he is forever at the mercy of the natives, down to the last inflection of the voice.

AFTER READING

1. Reread the text. As you read, **annotate** it: Underline things you think are significant, make notes in the margins, put question marks next to things that puzzle you, and so on. In other words, mark up the text in any way you wish. (See Appendix B.3, pp. 215–16, for an explanation and examples of annotating.)

   Exchange textbooks with a classmate. Talk about what you marked and why. Then discuss what you did with the class.

2. a. Reread the selection again. Make a **double-entry response**: Draw a line down the middle of the left page of your notebook. On the left side of the page, copy one or two sentences or ideas that interest you. On the right side of the page, write a response to what you wrote (your reactions, thoughts, ideas, associations, questions, feelings, and so on). (See Appendix B.2, p. 211, for more explanation.)

   b. Exchange notebooks with a classmate. Read what your classmate wrote, and respond to it in writing. (Write directly in your classmate's log, on the right-hand page of the notebook.)

   c. After reading your classmate's response to your entry, read your writing and your classmate's response to your group.

3. As a group, write a question you still have about the text. Discuss your question with the class.

HOW I READ IT

For what kinds of reading might annotating be useful? Talk about this question with the class.

HOW IT'S WRITTEN

1. Reread the text to find words or phrases that express or imply feelings or attitudes about being a foreigner. Work with a partner.

Use a pen to circle words that are *positive*; use a pencil (or pen with different-colored ink) to circle words that are *negative*.

2. Make two lists of the words, the positive and the negative. Compare your lists with others in the class. Talk about this:

Which list is longer, the positive or the negative?

What effect do these words have on you as a reader?

TOPICS FOR WRITING

Choose one activity.

Activity A: Notice that these three short notes are all related to the topic of being a foreigner, but they could also be read alone, as three separate pieces of writing. Write such a "note" of your own. The title can be "A Note on Being a Foreigner," or "A Note on Being _____."

Activity B: Some of Reid's statements can be considered opinions rather than facts; that is, they could be argued with. Find one such statement of opinion that you strongly agree or disagree with. Support your position with examples from the readings in this unit and from your own experience or the experience of other people you know or have read about.

Activity C: What connections, if any, do you see between what Reid says and what Liu and Mohm experienced? Explain the connections in writing.

AFTER WRITING

1. Exchange papers with a classmate. Write a response to your classmate's writing:
   a. What do you understand the important point to be?
   b. What do you like best about the piece?

2. Read your partner's comments. Then read your writing aloud to your group. As a group, pick one piece to read to the class.

About All the Readings in This Chapter

PREPARING FOR WRITING

1. In "Notes on Being a Foreigner," Reid classified foreigners into three kinds: foreigners by necessity, foreigners by accident, and foreigners by choice. In your group, decide which of these categories these people fall into: Iu-choi Chan or Bernardin Monestime, Annie John, Liu Zongren, Phat Mohm. For each person, support your classification with at least one reference to the readings.

2. a. Reread all of the entries in your reading log for this chapter.
   b. With the class, list some *issues* that arise when people leave one country or place and arrive in another. *Note:* An *issue* is a concern shared by many people. An issue can be stated in a few words (leaving home) or by questions (How do people feel when they leave home? Can people do anything to make leaving home easier?).
   c. Choose one or two issues from your class list, and make some *generalizations* about them. *Note:* A *generalization* is a judgment or observation that can apply to many similar people, things, or experiences. A generalization should be expressed in a complete sentence; for example:

   People who leave home have to cope with feelings of sadness.

   Some people, when leaving home, experience conflicting feelings, such as both relief and sadness.

TOPICS FOR WRITING

Choose one activity.

Activity A: Using Reid's classifications of foreigners (foreigners by necessity, by accident, by choice), explain in writing into which category some of these people fall: Iu-choi Chan or Bernardin Monestime, Annie John, Liu Zongren, Phat Mohm, and any other person you know or have read about. Support your writing with proof from the readings in this chapter and your experience or reading.

Activity B: Write down one *generalization* you can make about people leaving one place and arriving in a new place. Write a composition in which you support your generalization through examples from the readings in this chapter or from your own experience.

Activity C: Write a letter of advice to a friend who is moving to a new and different country or city. Tell the person what problems and feelings he or she might have when arriving and possible ways of coping. Use examples from the readings in this chapter and from your own experiences.

Activity D: Interview someone who has recently arrived here. Write that person's story. If you wish, compare that person's experiences to those of any of the people you read about in this chapter.

AFTER WRITING

1. Give your writing to two different people to read. These people should write reactions or responses to your writing in their reading log, just as they would for the readings in this book.

2. Read your readers' responses. Put your writing away for a day or two. Then reread it, asking yourself these questions:
   a. What point does this writing make? Is it clear?
   b. What do I like about the piece?
   c. How could it be improved?

3. Write about how you wrote this piece. For example, did you do anything different from what you did when writing the other pieces in this chapter? What changes could you make? (See Appendix D, p. 220, for more explanation.)

Extra Readings

Stopping by Woods on a Snowy Evening
Robert Frost

Robert Frost is a popular American poet who was born in 1875 and died in 1963. In the preface to one book of his poems, he wrote: "A poem begins in delight and ends in wisdom. . . . For me the initial delight is in the surprise of remembering something I didn't know I knew." Many of his readers find that true of his poems.

Whose woods these are I think I know.
His house is in the village though;
He will not see me stopping here
To watch his woods fill up with snow.

My little horse must think it queer
To stop without a farmhouse near
Between the woods and frozen lake
The darkest evening of the year.

He gives his harness bells a shake
To ask if there is some mistake.
The only other sound's the sweep
Of easy wind and downy flake.

The woods are lovely, dark and deep,
But I have promises to keep,
And miles to go before I sleep,
And miles to go before I sleep.

Stowaway

Armando Socarras Ramírez (as told to Denis Fodor and John Reddy)

Fidel Castro became prime minister of Cuba in 1959. At first he was admired by most Cubans as a dedicated revolutionary. Gradually, however, more and more people became disturbed by his close ties to the Soviet Union and began to leave the country. Many left legally; others found ways to escape. One teenager decided to try a unique method of escape. In "Stowaway," Armando Socarras Ramírez tells the story of his incredible flight from Cuba.

The jet engines of the Iberia Airlines DC-8 thundered in ear-splitting crescendo as the big plane taxied toward where we huddled in the tall grass just off the end of the runway at Havana's José Martí Airport. For months, my friend Jorge Pérez Blanco and I had been planning to stow away in a wheel well on this flight, No. 904—Iberia's once-weekly, nonstop run from Havana to Madrid. Now, in the late afternoon of June 3, 1970, our moment had come.

We realized that we were pretty young to be taking such a big gamble; I was seventeen, Jorge sixteen. But we were both determined to escape from Cuba, and our plans had been carefully made. We knew that departing airliners taxied to the end of the 11,500-foot runway, stopped momentarily after turning around, then roared at full throttle down the runway to take off. We wore rubber-soled shoes to aid us in crawling up the wheels and carried ropes to secure ourselves inside the wheel well. We had also stuffed cotton in our ears as protection against the shriek of the four jet engines. Now we lay sweating with fear as the massive craft swung into its about-face, the jet blast flattening the grass all around us. "Let's run!" I shouted to Jorge.

We dashed onto the runway and sprinted toward the left-hand wheels of the momentarily stationary plane. As Jorge began to scramble up the 42-inch-high tires, I saw there was not room for us both in the single well. "I'll try the other side!" I shouted. Quickly I climbed onto the right wheels, grabbed a strut, and, twisting and wriggling, pulled myself into the semi-dark well. The plane began rolling immediately, and I grabbed some machinery to keep from falling out. The roar of the engines nearly deafened me.

As we became airborne, the huge double wheels, scorching hot from takeoff, began folding into the compartment. I tried to flatten myself against the overhead as they came closer and closer; then, in desperation, I pushed at them with my feet. But they pressed powerfully upward, squeezing me terrifyingly against the roof of the well. Just when I felt that I would be crushed, the wheels locked in place and the bay doors beneath them closed, plunging me into darkness. So there I was, my five-foot-four-inch 140-pound frame literally wedged in amid a spaghettilike maze of conduits and machinery. I could not move enough to tie myself to anything, so I stuck my rope behind a pipe.

Then, before I had time to catch my breath, the bay doors suddenly dropped open again and the wheels stretched out into their landing position. I held on for dear life, swinging over the abyss, wondering if I had been spotted, if even now the plane was turning back to hand me over to Castro's police.

By the time the wheels began retracting again, I had seen a bit of extra space among all the machinery where I could safely squeeze. Now I knew there *was* room for me, even though I could scarcely breathe. After a few minutes, I touched one of the tires and found that it had cooled off. I swallowed some aspirin tablets against the head-splitting noise and began to wish that I had worn something warmer than my light sport shirt and green fatigues.

> Up in the cockpit of Flight 904, Captain Valentín Vara del Rey, forty-four, had settled into the routine of the overnight flight, which would last eight hours and twenty minutes. Takeoff had been normal, with the aircraft and its 147 passengers, plus a crew of 10, lifting off at 170 m.p.h. But right after lift-off, something unusual had happened. One of three red lights on the instrument panel had remained lighted, indicating improper retraction of the landing gear.
> "Are you having difficulty?" the control tower asked.
> "Yes," replied Vara del Rey. "There is an indication that the right wheel hasn't closed properly. I'll repeat the procedure."
> The captain relowered the landing gear, then raised it again. This time the red light blinked out.
> Dismissing the incident as a minor malfunction, the captain turned his attention to climbing to assigned cruising altitude. On leveling out, he observed that the temperature outside was 41 degrees F. Inside, the pretty stewardesses began serving dinner to the passengers.

Shivering uncontrollably from the bitter cold, I wondered if Jorge had made it into the other wheel well and began thinking about what had brought me to this desperate situation. I thought about my parents and my girl, María Esther, and wondered what they would think when they learned what I had done.

My father is a plumber, and I have four brothers and a sister. We are poor, like most Cubans. Our house in Havana has just one large room; eleven people live in it—or did. Food was scarce and strictly rationed. About the only fun I had was playing baseball and walking with María Esther along the seawall. When I turned sixteen, the government shipped me off to vocational school in Betancourt, a sugarcane village in Matanzas Province. There I was supposed to learn welding, but classes were often interrupted to send us off to plant cane.

Young as I was, I was tired of living in a state that controlled *everyone's* life. I dreamed of freedom. I wanted to become an artist and live in the United States, where I had an uncle. I knew that thousands of Cubans had got to America and done well there. As the time approached when I would be drafted, I thought more and more of trying to get away. But how? I knew that two planeloads of people are allowed to leave Havana for Miami each day, but there is a waiting list of eight hundred thousand for these flights. Also, if you sign up to leave, the government looks on you as a *gusano*—a worm—and life becomes even less bearable.

My hopes seemed futile. Then I met Jorge at a Havana baseball game. After the game we got to talking. I found out that Jorge, like myself, was disillusioned with Cuba. "The system takes away your freedom—forever," he complained.

Jorge told me about the weekly flight to Madrid. Twice we went to the airport to reconnoiter. Once a DC-8 took off and flew directly over us; the wheels were still down, and we could see into the well compartments. "There's enough room in there for me," I remember saying.

These were my thoughts as I lay in the freezing darkness more than five miles above the Atlantic Ocean. By now we had been in the air about an hour, and I was getting lightheaded from the lack of oxygen. Was it really only a few hours earlier that I had bicycled through the rain with Jorge and hidden in the grass? Was Jorge safe? My parents? María Esther? I drifted into unconsciousness.

The sun rose over the Atlantic like a great golden globe, its rays glinting off the silver-and-red fuselage of Iberia's DC-8 as it crossed the European coast high over Portugal. With the end of the 5,563-mile flight in sight, Captain Vara del Rey began his descent toward Madrid's Barajas Airport. Arrival would be at 8 A.M. local time, the captain told his passengers over the intercom, and the weather in Madrid was sunny and pleasant.

Shortly after passing over Toledo, Vara del Rey let down his landing gear. As always, the maneuver was accompanied by a buffeting as the wheels hit the slipstream and a 200-m.p.h. turbulence swirled through the wheel wells. Now the plane went into its final approach; now, a spurt of flame and smoke from the tires as the DC-8 touched down at about 140 m.p.h.

It was a perfect landing—no bumps. After a brief post-flight check, Vara del Rey walked down the ramp steps and stood by the nose of the plane waiting for a car to pick him up, along with his crew.

Nearby, there was a sudden, soft plop as the frozen body of Armando Socarras fell to the concrete apron beneath the plane. José Rocha Lorenzana, a security guard, was the first to reach the crumpled figure. "When I touched his clothes, they were frozen as stiff as wood," Rocha said. "All he did was make a strange sound, a kind of moan."

"I couldn't believe it at first," Vara del Rey said when told of Armando. "But then I went over to see him. He had ice over his nose and mouth. And his color . . ." As he watched the unconscious boy being bundled into a truck, the captain kept exclaiming to himself, "Impossible! Impossible!"

The first thing I remember after losing consciousness was hitting the ground at the Madrid airport. Then I blacked out again and woke up later at the Gran Hospital de la Beneficencia in downtown Madrid, more dead than alive. When they took my temperature, it was so low that it did not even register on the thermometer. "Am I in Spain?" was my first question. And then, "Where's Jorge?" (Jorge is believed to have been knocked down by the jet blast while trying to climb into the other wheel well, and to be in prison in Cuba.)

Doctors said later that my condition was comparable to that of a patient undergoing "deep freeze" surgery—a delicate process performed only under carefully controlled conditions. Dr. José María Pajares, who cared for me, called my survival a "medical miracle," and, in truth, I feel lucky to be alive.

A few days after my escape, I was up and around the hospital, playing cards with my police guard and reading stacks of letters from all over the world. I especially liked one from a girl in California. "You are a hero," she wrote, "but not very wise." My uncle, Elo Fernández, who lives in New Jersey, telephoned and invited me to come to the United States to live with him. The International Rescue Committee arranged my passage and has continued to help me.

I am fine now. I live with my uncle and go to school to learn English. I still hope to study to be an artist. I want to be a good citizen and contribute something to this country, for I love it here. You can smell freedom in the air.

I often think of my friend Jorge. We both knew the risk we were taking, and that we might be killed in our attempt to escape Cuba. But it seemed worth the chance. Even knowing the risks, I would try to escape again if I had to.

Moon Orchid's Arrival
Maxine Hong Kingston

In this part of Woman Warrior, *her autobiography, Maxine Hong Kingston refers to her mother as Brave Orchid and her mother's sister as Moon Orchid.*

When she was about sixty-eight years old, Brave Orchid took a day off to wait at San Francisco International Airport for the plane that was bringing her sister to the United States. She had not seen Moon Orchid for thirty years. She had begun this waiting at home, getting up a half-hour before Moon Orchid's plane took off in Hong Kong. Brave Orchid would add her will power to the forces that keep an airplane up. Her head hurt with the concentration. The plane had to be light, so no matter how tired she felt, she dared not rest her spirit on a wing but continuously and gently pushed up on the plane's belly. She had already been waiting at the airport for nine hours. She was wakeful.

Next to Brave Orchid sat Moon Orchid's only daughter, who was helping her aunt wait. Brave Orchid had made two of her own children come too because they could drive, but they had been lured away by the magazine racks and the gift shops and coffee shops. Her American children could not sit for very long. They did not understand sitting; they had wandering feet. She hoped they would get back from the pay t.v.'s or the pay toilets or wherever they were spending their money before the plane arrived. If they did not come back soon, she would go look for them. If her son thought he could hide in the men's room, he was wrong.

"Are you all right, Aunt?" asked her niece.

"No, this chair hurts me. Help me pull some chairs together so I can put my feet up."

She unbundled a blanket and spread it out to make a bed for herself. On the floor she had two shopping bags full of canned peaches, real peaches, beans wrapped in taro leaves, cookies, Thermos bottles, enough food for everybody, though only her niece would eat with her. Her bad boy and bad girl were probably sneaking hamburgers, wasting their money. She would scold them. . . .

Suddenly her son and daughter came running. "Come, Mother. The plane's landed early. She's here already." They hurried, folding up their mother's encampment. She was glad her children were not useless. They must have known what this trip to San Francisco was about then. "It's a good thing I made you come early," she said.

Brave Orchid pushed to the front of the crowd. She had to be in front. The passengers were separated from the people waiting for them by glass doors and walls. Immigration Ghosts were stamping papers. The travellers crowded along some conveyor belts to have their luggage searched. Brave Orchid did not see her sister anywhere. She stood watching for four hours. Her children left and came back. "Why don't you sit down?" they asked.

"The chairs are too far away," she said.

"Why don't you sit on the floor then?"

No, she would stand, as her sister was probably standing in a line she could not see from here. Her American children had no feelings and no memory.

To while away time, she and her niece talked about the Chinese passengers. These new immigrants had it easy. On Ellis Island the people were thin after forty days at sea and had no fancy luggage.

"That one looks like her," Brave Orchid would say.

"No, that's not her."

Ellis Island had been made out of wood and iron. Here everything was new plastic, a ghost trick to lure immigrants into feeling safe and spilling their secrets. Then the Alien Office could send them right back. Otherwise, why did they lock her out, not letting her help her sister answer questions and spell her name? At Ellis Island when the ghost asked Brave Orchid what year her husband had cut off his pigtail, a Chinese who was crouching on the floor motioned her not to talk. "I don't know," she had said. If it weren't for that Chinese man, she might not be here today, or her husband either. She hoped some Chinese, a janitor or a clerk, would look out for Moon Orchid. Luggage conveyors fooled immigrants into thinking the Gold Mountain was going to be easy.

Brave Orchid felt her heart jump—Moon Orchid. "There she is," she shouted. But her niece saw it was not her mother at all. And it shocked her to discover the woman her aunt was pointing out. This was a young woman, younger than herself, no older than Moon Orchid the day the sisters parted. "Moon Orchid will have changed a little, of course," Brave Orchid was saying. "She will have learned to wear western clothes." The woman wore a navy blue suit with a bunch of dark cherries at the shoulder.

"No, Aunt," said the niece. "That's not my mother."

"Perhaps not. It's been so many years. Yes, it is your mother. It must be. Let her come closer, and we can tell. Do you think she's too far away for me to tell, or is it my eyes getting bad?"

"It's too many years gone by," said the niece.

Brave Orchid turned suddenly—another Moon Orchid, this one a neat little woman with a bun. She was laughing at something the person ahead of her in line said. Moon Orchid was just like that, laughing at nothing. "I would be able to tell the difference if one of them would only come closer," Brave Orchid said with tears, which she did not wipe. Two children met the woman with the cherries, and she shook their hands. The other woman was met by a young man. They looked at each other gladly, then walked away side by side.

Up close neither one of those women looked like Moon Orchid at all. "Don't worry, Aunt," said the niece. "I'll know her."

"I'll know her too. I knew her before you did."

The niece said nothing, although she had seen her mother only five years ago. Her aunt liked having the last word.

Finally Brave Orchid's children quit wandering and drooped on a railing. Who knew what they were thinking? At last the niece called out, "I see her! I see her! Mother! Mother!" Whenever the doors parted, she shouted, probably embarrassing the American cousins, but she didn't care. She called out, "Mama! Mama!" until the crack in the sliding doors became too small to let in her voice. "Mama!" What a strange word in an adult voice. Many people turned to see what adult was calling, "Mama!" like a child. Brave Orchid saw an old, old woman jerk her head up, her little eyes blinking confusedly, a woman whose nerves leapt toward the sound any-time she heard "Mama!" Then she relaxed to her own business again. She was a tiny, tiny lady, very thin, with little fluttering hands, and her hair was in a gray knot. She was dressed in a gray wool suit; she wore pearls around her neck and in her earlobes. Moon Orchid *would* travel with her jewels showing. Brave Orchid momentarily saw, like a larger, younger outline around this old woman, the sister she had been waiting for. The familiar dim halo faded, leaving the woman so old, so gray. So old. Brave Orchid pressed against the glass. *That* old lady? Yes, that old lady facing the ghost who stamped her papers without questioning her was her sister. Then, without noticing her family, Moon Orchid walked smiling over to the Suitcase Inspector Ghost, who took her boxes apart, pulling out puffs of tissue. From where she was, Brave Orchid could not see what her sister had chosen to carry across the ocean. She wished her sister would look her way. Brave Orchid thought that if *she* were entering a new country, she would be at the windows. Instead Moon Orchid hovered over the unwrapping, surprised at each reappearance as if she were opening presents after a birthday party.

"Mama!" Moon Orchid's daughter kept calling. Brave Orchid said to her children, "Why don't you call your aunt too? Maybe she'll hear us if all of you call out together." But her children slunk away. Maybe that shame-face they so often wore was American politeness.

"Mama!" Moon Orchid's daughter called again, and this time her mother looked right at her. She left her bundles in a heap and came running. "Hey!" the Customs Ghost yelled at her. She went back to clear up her mess, talking inaudibly to her daughter all the while. Her daughter pointed toward Brave Orchid. And at last Moon Orchid looked at her—two old women with faces like mirrors.

Their hands reached out as if to touch the other's face, then returned to their own, the fingers checking the grooves in the forehead and along the side of the mouth. Moon Orchid, who never understood the gravity of things, started smiling and laughing, pointing at Brave Orchid. Finally Moon Orchid gathered up her stuff, strings hanging and papers loose, and met her sister at the door, where they shook hands, oblivious to blocking the way.

"You're an old woman," said Brave Orchid.

"Aiaa. *You're* an old woman."

"But you are really old. Surely, you can't say that about me. I'm not old the way you're old."

"But *you* really are old. You're one year older than I am."

"Your hair is white and your face all wrinkled."

"You're so skinny."

"You're so fat."

"Fat women are more beautiful than skinny women."

The children pulled them out of the doorway. One of Brave Orchid's children brought the car from the parking lot, and the other heaved the luggage into the trunk. They put the two old ladies and the niece in the back seat. All the way home—across the Bay Bridge, over the Diablo hills, across the San Joaquin River to the valley, the valley moon so white at dusk—all the way home, the two sisters exclaimed every time they turned to look at each other, "Aiaa! How old!"

Brave Orchid forgot that she got sick in cars, that all vehicles but palanquins made her dizzy. "You're so old," she kept saying. "How did you get so old?"

Brave Orchid had tears in her eyes. But Moon Orchid said, "You look older than I. You *are* older than I," and again she'd laugh. "You're wearing an old mask to tease me." It surprised Brave Orchid that after thirty years she could still get annoyed at her sister's silliness.

Chapter 2

Two Worlds

1. The title of this chapter is "Two Worlds."

   a. In your reading log, freewrite for a few minutes about the title of this chapter, "Two Worlds."
   b. Reread what you wrote.
   c. Write one sentence that summarizes the dominant idea of your freewrite (the kernel idea).
   d. Now either freewrite again for 5 minutes about the sentence you wrote in part (c), or write that sentence in the middle of a piece of paper and **cluster** words or phrases around it. (See Appendix A.2, pp. 204–205, for more explanation and examples of clustering.)

2. Read your second freewrite or show and explain your clustering to a partner. Tell each other what the most important point of the writing seems to be. How does your important point relate to the title of the chapter, "Two Worlds"?

BEFORE READING

1. An old song says, "Any place I hang my hat is home." How do you define "home"? How do you know when you're home? Do **clustering** for a few minutes in your reading log about the word *home*. (See Appendix A.2, pp. 204–205, for further explanation and examples of clustering.) Share your cluster with a partner.

2. Read the introductory information and "Sometimes Home Is Not Really Home" by Maggie Mok.

Sometimes Home Is Not Really Home
Maggie Mok

Maggie Mok was a student at Hunter College of the City University of New York when she wrote this composition.

I was born in Hong Kong, but most of us in Hong Kong consider that our real homes are on Mainland China. It may be only a small village in China. With all my desires and hopes alive, I went back to my "real home," a village in Canton, five years ago. Afterwards, I felt like I had landed on another planet rather than back home.

The first moment I stepped off the train, the people in the village looked at me as if I were a foreigner. A man came forward to ask me if I wanted to buy this or that. A woman suggested many inns for my stay. A group of children followed me. I felt like I was "E.T., come home."

I met my relatives at the station. It seemed that all my relatives had come to receive me. All of a sudden, I felt I was very important. But the first question my uncle asked me was how much money I had brought with me. Then my aunt asked me if I had brought any presents for them. I thought that I had made a wrong decision to come back to my "real home." I really wanted to step on the train and go back to Hong Kong.

In fact, I had planned to stay in the village for a week. After the first day of my visit, I decided to stay for only three days. As a matter of fact, even during that time, I seldom went out.

AFTER READING

1. Choose one activity. (Make sure at least one person in your group does each activity.)

   Activity A: What did Maggie Mok learn from her experience? In your reading log, make a list of the things she learned and share it with a partner.

   Activity B: What advice do you think Maggie Mok would give to a friend in Hong Kong who was planning to make a similar trip to Mainland China? Freewrite in your reading log and share your writing with a partner.

   Activity C: Do some research in the library and find out:

   a. Where is Hong Kong located in relation to Mainland China?
   b. What is the political status of Hong Kong now?
   c. How did it become that way?
   d. How will Hong Kong's relationship to China change in the future?

2. Tell your group what you learned.

HOW IT'S WRITTEN

Work with a partner.

1. There are four paragraphs in Maggie Mok's composition. Make a **descriptive outline** of the composition. That is, describe what each paragraph *says* (What information does it contain?) and what each paragraph *does* (What is its function?). Some things paragraphs do are introduce an idea, develop a reason, give an example, describe, list, compare, analyze, offer a hypothesis, explain, elaborate, synthesize, and conclude. (See Appendix B.4, pp. 217–18, for more explanation and an example of descriptive outlining.)

2. What connections do you see between the four paragraphs? List the words or ideas that hold the composition together and make it easy for the reader to move from one paragraph to the next.

3. Discuss your ideas with your group. Make a list of things to remember the next time you write a composition. Share your list with the

whole class. Write a combined list on the chalkboard. Copy any new ideas you want to remember into your reading log.

HOW I READ IT

1. Write for a few minutes in your log about how doing a descriptive outline about Maggie Mok's writing affected the way you read it.
2. Share your ideas with a partner.

TOPICS FOR WRITING

Choose one activity.

Activity A: Maggie Mok writes that when she saw all of her relatives waiting to greet her, she felt very important until she realized they were hoping she had brought them either money or gifts. Write about a time in your life when you arrived somewhere and were disappointed. What did you learn from this experience?

Activity B: Describe a situation in which people are living in a place they don't consider their home. Give the historical background of the place. Describe its relationship to the place people call home. Then tell what happens when someone travels from one place to the other, as Maggie Mok did.

Activity C: If you have seen the movie *E.T., the Extra-Terrestrial*, write a composition about how E.T.'s experience on Earth is similar to or different from an experience you have had in a new place.

AFTER WRITING

1. Exchange papers with a partner. Ask your partner to write a **descriptive outline** of your composition, as you did for Maggie Mok's for How It's Written, item 1. That is, describe what each paragraph *says* and what each paragraph *does*. (See Appendix B.4, pp. 217–18, for more explanation and an example of descriptive outlining.)

2. Look at the descriptive outline your partner did of your writing.

3. Write in your log about *how* you wrote this composition. For example, how did you decide what order to follow? Would you change anything after seeing your partner's descriptive outline? Why?

BEFORE READING

1. Read the title of the poem. Why do you think the title is a list of four words? Does love belong in that list? Why or why not? Freewrite in your log for 5 minutes.

2. Read the introductory information and the poem.

Exile and Orphanhood and Bitterness and Love

This poem is translated from a group of folk songs traditionally sung by women at funerals in the eighteenth and nineteenth centuries in Greece.

Exile and orphanhood and bitterness and love—
they weighed all four, and found that exile was the heaviest.
The exile in a foreign land should wear all black
to match the lava-blackness of his heart.

AFTER READING

1. Do you agree with the writer that exile is "the heaviest"? Write a response in your reading log.

2. Did reading the introductory information change the way you read this poem? How is being in exile like being in mourning? Talk about this with your group.

HOW I READ IT

1. Write for a few minutes in your log about how reading a poem is different from reading another student's composition or a short story.

2. Discuss your ideas with your group.

TOPICS FOR WRITING

Choose one activity.

Activity A: Choose one word in the title of the poem other than *exile*. Start with the first line of the poem as it is, and write three more sentences or paragraphs about the word you chose.

Activity B: With a partner, make a list of emotions, and decide what color clothing people who feel those emotions would wear. Either turn your list into a poem, or write a short paragraph about each color, describing the person wearing it.

Activity C: The author of the poem says that exile is "the heaviest." Do you agree or disagree? Write a composition either agreeing or disagreeing with the writer, supporting your opinion with reasons and examples from your experience, the experience of people you know, or your reading. (*Note*: Reread what you wrote for After Reading 1 before starting your composition.)

AFTER WRITING

Read your writing to your group. Choose one poem or composition from the group to read aloud to the whole class.

BEFORE READING

1. Read the introductory information.
2. Copy the first sentence of "A Story of Conflicts" into your reading log.
3. Write down three questions that you hope will be answered in "A Story of Conflicts."
4. Read "A Story of Conflicts."

A Story of Conflicts
Yeghia Aslanian

Yeghia Aslanian came to the United States in 1979 and received a doctorate in TESOL (teaching English to speakers of other languages) from Teachers College, Columbia University, in New York City. He now teaches at the Borough of Manhattan Community College of the City University of New York.

Armenians Christians, language

Mine is a story of conflicts. I was born into an Armenian (consequently Christian) family in Isfahan, Iran, a town with a predominantly Islamic culture. I had to cope with the stigma of being a "bad" Armenian or a "dirty" Armenian (depending on who was doing the cursing). Although by the 1960s and '70s you could see Armenians in socially prominent positions, when I was a child we were often looked upon as an alien ethnic group who were not supposed to mingle with Muslims. There was a separate Armenian section of Isfahan, but because the language of instruction at elementary school was Persian (or Farsi), I had two languages and two cultures to grapple with. Having to struggle to catch up with classmates whose mother tongue was Persian, I felt Armenian to be a hindrance to my social progress and social image. As soon as I'd open my mouth to say something, they'd know I was not one of them, so the conversation would end right there and then.

Childhood humiliation can make or break a person; it made me. When I realized that my social image was at stake, at school or in the street, I plotted against myself. I began to devote myself to Persian—reading, copying and memorizing long stretches of Persian texts. I studied my school subjects day in and day out and managed in this way to get a head start over my classmates, rehashing what I had learned for those of them not in the mood to apply themselves. Little by little, I gained acceptance at school—at the expense of my Armenian.

During my first six years of school, I had lessons in Armenian only a few hours a week. In high school the situation was worse, for it was a government school and I was taught no Armenian at all. My Armenian identity was increasingly subjugated. The only place I had a slight possibility of using Armenian was at home—if there was anything parents and children could talk about in a cultural milieu in which children were supposed to be seen and not heard.

My parents were functionally illiterate in Persian, and so if I read a doctor's prescription (which was always in Persian) for them, they considered me worthy of all the money they'd spent on me and all the troubles they'd endured for me. I always suspect that my desire for learning was a response to my parents' being illiterate. That I graduated from school with honors heightened their confidence in me, and it also made it clear to me that I could maintain my self-esteem in my little world without Armenian. And yet, because I had not achieved the proficiency in my parents' language that other Armenian students normally acquired by high school, if I ran into a friend who "knew" Armenian, I'd feel inferior to him. The two languages and the two cultures were tearing me apart.

When it was time to go to the university, I stayed awake many a night pondering my future. What to do? Wishing to preserve both my self and my image, I could not choose between my two equally powerful cultural heritages, in both of which I thought I had somehow failed. An answer presented itself in English, which I had studied as a foreign language in high school, with enough success so that from the very beginning I thought, or at least my teachers thought, that I had a special ability for languages. In fact, the pull of English had been so irresistible that I enrolled in a night school to study it further. Now, thinking it would resolve my dilemma, I made English language and literature my undergraduate major. I devoted myself completely to this third route, shutting off the other two, except for the occasional required course in Persian and answering some friends' letters in Armenian. I felt great relief and was finally at peace with myself. Or was I?

I received a BA in English language and literature from Tehran University, an MA in Teaching English as a Second Language from the American University in Beirut, and a doctorate from Columbia's Teachers College in Teaching English to Speakers of Other Languages. But when I finished this last degree, I realized that I wasn't at peace with my English identity either, that abandoning the two worlds that had formed me had cost [caused] me excruciating pain, and that to be truly happy with myself I had to recapture the Armenian and Persian languages. I made up my mind to regain my origins. I began to read, write, and translate from English to Persian and vice versa. I opened my long-forgotten Armenian books—I have very few of them!—reading them very slowly. And as I've grown a bit more comfortable, I've started reading Armenian classic and modern literature. I feel I'm coming alive again.

If all goes well, my daughter will have to learn four languages: English, Armenian, Italian (my wife is Italian), and Persian. I think the idea of using only English in this country ignores the cultural wealth and linguistic variety that immigrants have always brought with them. A society like this one should be able to tolerate differences and make the best of them. I'm aware of how our ESL students are enriched by their struggle to learn a new language and adapt to a new culture at the same time they work to preserve their own heritage. I myself rarely miss the two weekly one-hour radio programs in Armenian and Persian on WEVD, "the station that speaks your language." And as I try hard to grow in my three languages and cultures, I find my inner conflicts gradually subsiding. Or at least I think so, and thinking is a reality.

AFTER READING

Choose one activity. (Make sure each activity is done by at least one person in your group.)

Activity A: Look up these words in a large dictionary or encyclopedia: *Armenian, Christian, Islamic, Muslim, Persian, Farsi*. Does more information on these words make the story clearer? Report to your group.

Activity B: The writer says, "Childhood humiliation can make or break a person." What associations do you have with these words? How do the associations make you feel? In your reading log, write for 10 minutes about any similar childhood experiences you or someone you know may have had. Share your writing with your group.

HOW I READ IT

1. Compare the questions you asked in Before Reading 3 with those of the other members of your group.

2. Discuss with your group how asking these specific questions changed the way you read "A Story of Conflicts."

HOW IT'S WRITTEN

1. Work with a partner. Choose one activity.

   Activity A: Trace the writer's attitude toward his own culture, Armenian, from the first paragraph to the last by underlining words or phrases that show how it changes. Describe how the writer's attitude changes in a summary sentence.

   Activity B: The first sentence of this reading is "Mine is a story of conflicts." How many conflicts are described in this piece? Reread the piece, and list the conflicts described in their order of importance for the writer. How did you decide which ones are most important? What order did the writer put them in?

2. Share your findings with your group. Discuss what you have learned from these activities about ordering a story that you could apply to your own writing. Then try to trace the development of an idea or list the main ideas in order of importance in a piece of writing from one of your group members.

TOPICS FOR WRITING

Choose one activity.

Activity A: The writer says, "Childhood humiliation can make or break a person." Write about a time when you were or someone you know was humiliated as a child. Describe the incident in detail, and tell what the consequences were. Did it make or break you or your friend? How do you know? (*Note*: If you did Activity B in After Reading, refer to what you wrote in your reading log.)

Activity B: The writer says that the reason he was so committed to education was that his parents didn't know how to read and write. Write about a time when someone else's inability to do something inspired you or someone you know to learn to do it. Tell the story in chronological order, as this writer did.

Activity C: The writer says, "The two languages and the two cultures were tearing me apart." Write about a time when you experienced a conflict or an inability to make a choice between two things.

AFTER WRITING

1. Read your writing to your group. Ask your group to tell you:
   a. The development of your ideas and the order you put them in
   b. If there is another order you could use to make your writing clearer

2. Write in your log about *how* you wrote this composition. For example, how did you get ideas? How did you decide what order to use? Did your group's feedback surprise you? In what ways?

BEFORE READING

1. Read the introductory information.
2. Write in your reading log for 5 minutes about a strong emotional attachment you have had to someone.
3. Read your writing to your group. Notice if your group members describe their attachments in positive or negative terms.
4. Read "No Longer One of Them."

No Longer One of Them
Vivian Gornick

Fierce Attachments, *by Vivian Gornick, is the story of the writer's lifelong, intensely intimate relationship with her mother. This episode is about the beginning of Gornick's career as a student at City College, one of the four-year colleges of the City University of New York.*

I lived among my people, but I was no longer one of them.

I think this was true for most of us at City College. We still used the subways, still walked the familiar streets between classes, still returned to the neighborhood each night, talked to our high-school friends, and went to sleep in our own beds. But secretly we had begun to live in a world inside our heads where we read, talked, thought in a way that separated us from our parents, the life of the house and that of the street. We had been initiated, had learned the difference between hidden and expressed thought. This made us subversives in our own homes.

As thousands before me have said, "For us it was City College or nothing." I enjoyed the solidarity those words invoked but rejected the implied deprivation. At City College I sat talking in a basement cafeteria until ten or eleven at night with a half dozen others who also never wanted to go home to Brooklyn or the Bronx, and here in the cafeteria my education took root. Here I learned that Faulkner was America, Dickens was politics, Marx was sex, Jane Austen was the idea of culture, that I came from a ghetto and D. H. Lawrence was a visionary. Here my love of literature named itself, and amazement over the life of the mind blossomed. I discovered that people were transformed by ideas, and that intellectual conversation was immensely erotic.

We never stopped talking. Perhaps because we did very little else (restricted by sexual fear and working-class economics, we didn't go to the theater and we didn't make love), but certainly we talked so much because most of us had been reading in bottled-up silence from the age of six on and City College was our great release. It was not from the faculty that City drew its reputation for intellectual goodness, it was from its students, it was from us. Not that we were intellectually distinguished, we weren't; but our hungry energy vitalized the place. The idea of intellectual life burned in us. While we pursued ideas we felt known, to ourselves and to one another. The world made sense, there was ground beneath our feet, a place in the universe to stand. City College made conscious in me inner cohesion as a first value.

I think my mother was very quickly of two minds about me and City, although she had wanted me to go to school, no question about that, had been energized by the determination that I do so (instructed me in the middle of her first year of widowhood to enter the academic, not the commercial, course of high-school study), and was even embattled when it became something of an issue in the family.

"Where is it written that a working-class widow's daughter should go to college?" one of my uncles said to her, drinking coffee at our kitchen table on a Saturday morning in my senior year in high school.

"Here it is written," she had replied, tapping the table hard with her middle finger. "Right here it is written. The girl goes to college."

"Why?" he had pursued.

"Because I say so."

"But why? What do you think will come of it?"

"I don't know. I only know she's clever, she deserves an education, and she's going to get one. This is America. The girls are not cows in the field only waiting for a bull to mate with." I stared at her. Where had *that* come from? My father had been dead only five years, she was in full widowhood swing.

The moment was filled with conflict and bravado. She felt the words she spoke but she did not mean them. She didn't even know what she meant by an education. When she discovered at my graduation that I wasn't a teacher she acted as though she'd been swindled. In her mind a girl child went in one door marked college and came out another marked teacher.

"You mean you're not a teacher?" she said to me, eyes widening as her two strong hands held my diploma down on the kitchen table.

"No," I said.

"What have you been doing there all these years?" she asked quietly.

"Reading novels," I replied.

She marveled silently at my chutzpah.

But it wasn't really a matter of what I could or could not do with the degree. We were people who knew how to stay alive, she never doubted I would find a way. No, what drove her, and divided us, was me thinking. She hadn't understood that going to school meant I would start thinking: coherently and out loud. She was taken by violent surprise. My sentences got longer within a month of those first classes. Longer, more complicated, formed by words whose meaning she did not always know. I had never before spoken a word she didn't know. Or made a sentence whose logic she couldn't follow. Or attempted an opinion that grew out of an abstraction. It made her crazy. Her face began to take on a look of animal cunning when I started a sentence that could not possibly be concluded before three clauses hit the air. Cunning sparked anger, anger flamed into rage. "What are you talking about?" she would shout at me. "What *are* you talking about? Speak English, please! We all understand English in this house. Speak it!"

Her response stunned me. I didn't get it. Wasn't she pleased that I could say something she didn't understand? Wasn't that what it was all about? I was the advance guard. I was going to take her into the new world. All she had to do was adore what I was becoming, and here she was refusing. I'd speak my new sentences, and she would turn on me as though I'd performed a vile act right there at the kitchen table.

She, of course, was as confused as I. She didn't know why she was angry, and if she'd been told she was angry she would have denied it, would have found a way to persuade both herself and any interested listener that she was proud I was in school, only why did I have to be such a showoff? Was that what going to college was all about? Now, take Mr. Lewis, the insurance agent, an educated man if ever there was one, got a degree from City College in 1929, 1929 mind you, and never made you feel stupid, always spoke in simple sentences, but later you thought about what he said. That's the way an educated person should talk. Here's this snotnose kid coming into the kitchen with all these big words, sentences you can't make head or tail of . . .

I was seventeen, she was fifty. I had not yet come into my own as a qualifying belligerent but I was a respectable contender and she, naturally, was at the top of her game. The lines were drawn, and we did not fail one another. Each of us rose repeatedly to the bait the other one tossed out. Our storms shook the apartment: paint blistered on the wall, linoleum cracked on the floor, glass shivered in the window frame. We barely kept our hands off one another, and more than once we approached disaster.

One Saturday afternoon she was lying on the couch. I was reading in a nearby chair. Idly she asked, "What are you reading?" Idly I replied, "A comparative history of the idea of love over the last three hundred years." She looked at me for a moment. "That's ridiculous," she said slowly. "Love is love. It's the same everywhere, all the time. What's to compare?" "That's absolutely not true," I shot back. "You don't know what you're talking about. It's only an idea, Ma. That's all love is. Just an idea. You think it's a function of the mysterious immutable being, but it's not! There is, in fact, no such thing as the mysterious immutable being . . ." Her legs were off the couch so fast I didn't see them go down. She made fists of her hands, closed her eyes tight, and howled, "I'll kill you-u-u! Snake in my bosom, I'll kill you. How dare you talk to me that way?" And then she was coming at me. She was small and chunky. So was I. But I had thirty years on her. I was out of the chair faster than her arm could make contact, and running, running through the apartment, racing for the bathroom, the only room with a lock on it. The top half of the bathroom door was a panel of frosted glass. She arrived just as I turned the lock, and couldn't put the brakes on. She drove her fist through the glass, reaching for me. Blood, screams, shattered glass on both sides of the door. I thought that afternoon, one of us is going to die of this attachment.

AFTER READING

1. Reread the text, *annotating* it. Underline things you think are significant, make notes in the margins, put question marks next to things that puzzle you, and so on. (See Appendix B.3, pp. 215–16, for more explanation and examples of annotating.)

2. When you finish, look back at all of the annotations you made, and write a paragraph summarizing them. Share your annotations and your paragraph with your group.

3. In "No Longer One of Them," Gornick writes that going to college changed her, made her different from her family and high school friends. She and her college friends began secretly living "in a world inside our heads." This difference, however, did not remain a secret because it was revealed by her language. With a partner, look back at "No Longer One of Them" and outline, on a new page, the development of her difference from her family and old friends and how that difference reveals itself in her language. How does she feel about being different from her family? How do you know? Discuss these questions with the whole class.

HOW IT'S WRITTEN

In describing how "fierce" her attachment to her mother is, Gornick emphasizes the sense of touch. Starting with the paragraph that begins "I was seventeen, she was fifty," underline the words that appeal to the sense of touch. Talk with your group about how you might make your own writing more powerful by appealing to the reader's senses.

TOPICS FOR WRITING

Choose one activity.

Activity A: Write a composition about people who grow up to be different from the other members of their family. Begin with a generalization. (See page 32 for an explanation of generalizations.) To support your generalization, use examples from Gornick's story, your own life, the lives of other people you know, or other readings.

Activity B: Gornick experiences conflict, both internal and external. Write a composition about conflict in which you compare or contrast her conflicts with your own or someone else's you know. (*Note*: If you chose Activity C of Topics for Writing in the section on "A Story of Conflicts," page 55, reread it now and see if you can use it as an example in this composition.)

Activity C: Write a true story called "A Fierce Attachment" about an intense emotional relationship you have or have had with someone in your family in which there is a conflict. At the end of your composition, write what you have learned from your experience or what advice you would give others in a similar situation. Try to appeal to the reader's senses, particularly the sense of touch, to make your writing more powerful. (*Note*: Start by looking back at what you wrote in your reading log about Gornick's appeals to the senses.)

AFTER WRITING

1. Exchange papers with a classmate who is not a member of your regular group. Write responses to each other's writing: What will you remember about your classmate's piece?

2. Read your writing aloud to your group. As a group, choose one piece of writing to read aloud to the whole class.

BEFORE READING

1. Read the introductory information and title.

2. Crespo's composition was written in response to a topic that stated that immigrants to the United States should give up speaking their native language and practicing the traditions of their native culture when they arrive. It went on to say that they should learn English and adapt to American culture as quickly as possible. Then it asked the writer to write a composition agreeing or disagreeing with this idea.

   With a partner, discuss whether you think Crespo agreed or disagreed with this topic. What do you base your guess on?

3. Read "Private Language."

Private Language
Patty Crespo

Patty Crespo came to the United States from Ecuador in 1983 to study at Hunter College of the City University of New York. She wrote this composition in 50 minutes to pass the final examination of an ESL writing course. At the time she wrote it, Crespo could not decide if she wanted to stay in the United States or return to Ecuador.

The United States of America is one of the biggest countries in the world. It's famous because of its freedom and rights of liberty. It is well-known because its population comes from all over the world. The immigrants can learn the United States' language, English, to keep this country united, but it is unfair to change their culture for an American way of life.

I believe that recent immigrants should learn English in order to live in this country. They should learn the "public language" to make a better living. If they don't learn English, they won't be able to communicate and do what they want. For example, my mother's friend came here from Ecuador three years ago. She doesn't speak English. One day her daughter, Anita, couldn't breathe. She didn't know what was going on, but she told her mother to call an ambulance. When her mother called the hospital, she couldn't talk. The operator couldn't understand what Anita's mother was saying. Thank God, her sister arrived and called the ambulance. The doctor told her sister that if she hadn't arrived at the hospital on time, Anita could have died. A pill had gotten stuck in her throat.

Immigrants should learn English to speak with the public, but they should also keep their language at home. The children of immigrants should learn how to speak their parents' language. It's very important to communicate with our relatives and family, in general. If we learn English only and forget our "private language," we won't be able to communicate with our parents. For example, Florence, my co-worker, speaks English only. Her mother didn't teach her Spanish (her mother language). Nowadays, Florence can't communicate with her grandparents or other relatives in Puerto Rico. She has lost her mother's language, tradition and culture.

Immigrants may replace their language with English, but it's unfair to give up their culture. They grow up with a way of living and it is difficult to change it because they are in another country. They have the right to keep their culture and values. We immigrants have the right to know where we come from and what our family's culture is. In this way, we can transmit it to our future generation. After all, one amendment of the constitution of this country gives us the right. It is freedom of religion, culture and speech.

In conclusion, immigrants should learn English in order to communicate with the public and to keep the country united, but they shouldn't exchange their culture for an American way of life. They have the right to keep it and transmit it to their future generation.

AFTER READING

Crespo has written what is usually called a persuasive or argumentative composition. That is, she tries to persuade the reader to consider her point of view as correct. Write her main idea at the top of a page. Then make a list of the reasons or examples she uses to support it. Put a star (*) next to the ones you think are especially persuasive.

Talk to your group about your lists. Which do you think are stronger, Crespo's reasons or her examples?

HOW IT'S WRITTEN

1. Work with a partner. Choose one activity.

   Activity A: Is Crespo arguing in favor of immigrants' keeping two languages, or is she arguing in favor of immigrants' keeping two cultures? Reread each paragraph. If the paragraph is about keeping two languages, write "language" in the margin. If it is about keeping two cultures, write, "culture."

   Activity B: How did Crespo draw from her own experience, from others' experience, and from her reading? Reread each paragraph, and write in the margin "her experience," "others' experience," and "reading."

2. Discuss your findings with your group.

HOW I READ IT

1. Reread the guess you made about whether Crespo would agree or disagree with the topic as it was stated.

2. Discuss with your group how writing down your guess changed the way you read the composition.

TOPICS FOR WRITING

Choose one activity.

Activity A: In this composition, Crespo says that her co-worker, Florence, can't communicate with her grandparents or other relatives in Puerto Rico because she doesn't speak her mother's native language, Spanish. Write about someone you know who is in a similar situation. Describe one incident in that person's life that made the person feel like an orphan or an exile.

Activity B: Write a story, real or imaginary, called "Private Language."

Activity C: Write a composition about the same topic Patty Crespo did. Persuade your reader, starting with a generalization and using reasons and examples, as Crespo did, that your opinion is one the reader should share. Notice how Crespo gives reasons and specific examples to support her argument. Be sure to do the same.

AFTER WRITING

1. Exchange compositions with a partner. List all of the reasons and examples in the composition in a column down the left side of the page. Write at least one specific question you would like to have answered about each one.

2. Write in your log in response to your partner's questions.

About All the Readings in This Chapter

PREPARING FOR WRITING

1. Choose one activity.

   Activity A: In many of the readings in this chapter, statements are made about the relationship between education, language, parents, conflict, and intimacy. Look back through all of them, and find places where the relationships between two or more of these ideas are expressed. On a page of your reading log, use clustering to show the relationships between those ideas.

   Activity B: In "A Story of Conflicts," "No Longer One of Them," and "Private Language," the language used at home is different from the language used outside the home. List other things that are different at home and outside the home in these readings.

2. As a group or class, make a list of the issues that were raised in these readings. (See page 32 for further explanation of *issue*.) Make a list of questions about those issues that could be answered in a composition.

TOPICS FOR WRITING

Choose one activity.

Activity A: Write a question you could ask about how education or language affects our relationships with family members. Use this question as your topic. Answer it in writing. You may use examples from the readings in this chapter and from your own experience. Write for someone who has not read this book and does not know about your experience.

Activity B: Find one issue or question that interests you in Preparing for Writing 2. Write about it using material from the readings, from your writing about the readings, and from your clustering of ideas. Write the composition for someone who has not read this book.

Activity C: All of the writers in this chapter are living and can be reached by writing to the publishers of their original books. Write a letter to one of them describing what you liked about their writing and asking questions about things you would like to know more about. Ask questions you really want answers to, since writers often respond to letters from their readers.

AFTER WRITING

1. Before you exchange your paper with someone, go over it carefully with your pen in hand, reading each word aloud so that your ear can hear it and touching each word with your pen. This proofreading technique should help you find errors. Don't stop until you find at least three things you want to change.

2. Give your composition to two people to read together. Ask these people to write a **descriptive outline** of your composition, stating what each paragraph says and what each paragraph does. (See Appendix B.4, pp. 217–18, for more explanation and an example of descriptive outlining.)

Extra Readings

old age sticks
e. e. cummings

e. e. cummings is a twentieth-century American poet. His poetry doesn't abide by the conventions of grammar and punctuation, but once unscrambled, the reader is often surprised and touched by its meaning.

old age sticks
up Keep
Off
signs) &

youth yanks them
down(old
age
cries No

Tres) & (pas)
youth laughs
(sing
old age

scolds Forbid
den Stop
Must
n't Don't

&) youth goes
right on
gr
owing old

Family Conflicts
Al Santoli

In a book called New Americans, *Al Santoli presents oral histories of recent immigrants and refugees in the United States. One of the families he interviewed was from Viet Nam. Trong Nguyen and his wife Thanh started a new life in Chicago in 1976. They worked hard to support their family and to improve their neighborhood in the center of Chicago's Uptown. Despite their successes, however, Trong and Thanh still talk of conflicts within their own family. They and their son Tran tell part of their story in this excerpt from "Uptown."*

TRONG: When my wife and I came to Chicago, our major concern was to feed our five small children. We had Vietnamese pride and did not want to take public aid. We wanted the American community and authorities to respect us. . . .

My son, Tran, was nine years old, and my daughters were five, four, three, and one. My two oldest children had a lot of problems with their classmates in Chicago. The school in Albany Park was a mixture of white, black, Asian, everything. Tran was beaten sometimes, and his teacher wasn't patient with him, because he didn't know English. I went to the school and told the principal that I thought the teacher was being unfair. The principal was sympathetic and said, "I understand." After that there was no more problem. . . .

After I saw the neighborhood begin to turn around and living conditions for the refugees improve, I thought, "How about their moral and cultural life?" There are family conflicts, because the children are learning so quickly in school to adopt American culture. The parents might learn a little English at work, but it is a very slow process. They have to rely a lot on the children. The kids watch television and forget about the Vietnamese cultural values. The parents are shocked. They feel they have lost authority. There are arguments. The children want to move out or run away. . . .

My own children like the new fashions, the New Wave. I've tried to stay with the Asian Confucian tradition. As a father, I have to be strict. But in this society, you can't force children to do what you say. They have their own lives.

THANH: Our children were very young when we came here. So we have adjusted and let them have some freedom. We realize that we can't live the way we did in Vietnam. But we try to teach them to respect family life. I tell my children, "The U.S. is liberal. You have the right to drive a car. But when you see a 'One Way' sign, you can't ignore it and say, 'This is a free country, nobody can tell me what to do.' That will lead to a bad accident where you can get hurt. You must also think that way in terms of family rules."

TRONG: Our oldest daughter is fifteen. I wouldn't be happy if a boy asked her to a dance at school or for a date, but it would be okay to go to a party at school, because it would be under supervision. Sometimes we compromise and allow her to go to a party at a friend's house if we know the parents.

Vietnamese tradition is not as strict with boys. I gave my son more freedom when he was in high school, but I had to know where he was going and who he was associating with. I told him, "I give you freedom, but you have to be home by 10:00 P.M., or midnight." If he didn't come home at the time limit—"Sorry," the next time he asks. But sometimes, when he was having a lot of fun and wanted to stay out a little longer, if he called me to ask permission, that was fine.

Last year, after Tran graduated from high school, he moved out on his own. That was a great shock for me. We didn't have enough money to send him to college, so he started working full-time to save for tuition. His high-school grades were average, but he is very artistic, a good drummer. In his free time, he practices a lot with his band. During days he works at a company downtown, and in the evenings he comes into our restaurant to help. . . .

TRAN: I didn't know what I wanted after I finished high school last year. My dad wanted me to go to college, but first I wanted to support myself. I moved out on my own because I wanted to have more life experience.

Now I live in this neighborhood, on the street next to the restaurant. A guy from my band rooms with me. . . .

There has been some conflict in my family because I want to establish myself on my own. But my loyalty to them hasn't changed. When I lived at home, I argued with my parents a lot. I had an attitude just like American kids. But once I left, I realized how much I respect them.

Before I moved back to the Uptown area, I practically forgot the Vietnamese language. I was eight or nine years old when we left Vietnam. When we came to America, I had to concentrate on learning the new language. In high school there were only two Vietnamese kids, so I hung out with American kids. There were a lot of different groups that kids hung around in. There were the jocks; the wimps, who always studied; the burnouts, who partied all the time. Each group never associated with the others. I like to hang around with all groups. I don't care if they're the wimps or the Melvins. But some kids' attitudes were, "You be with my group only, or we don't want you around." So I said, "Forget it. I don't need no one."

For all four years of high school, what I mostly did was go to school and come straight home. I'd listen to music, study, and play my drums. At that time, I really hated the Vietnamese—I don't know why. I played with only American kids, even though I didn't have many friends. Now that I'm back in Uptown, I like the Vietnamese better. Friendships with people here are a lot easier, even though the neighborhood is rough. . . .

TRONG: I was very upset when my son went out on his own. I was worried about his well-being. In the Vietnamese community, I saved a lot of families from the generation gap, but when the problem came to my own family, I couldn't solve it.

My children were very young when they came here, so their values have become much more American. I try to behave as an American too, but in my heart I am always Vietnamese.

Homework
Peter Cameron

Peter Cameron grew up in Pompton Plains, New Jersey, and currently works for a land conservation agency in New York City. His short stories have appeared in many magazines and anthologies.

My dog, Keds, was sitting outside of the A&P last Thursday when he got smashed by some kid pushing a shopping cart. At first we thought he just had a broken leg, but later we found out he was bleeding inside. Every time he opened his mouth, blood would seep out like dull red words in a bad silent dream.

Every night before my sister goes to her job she washes her hair in the kitchen sink with beer and mayonnaise and eggs. Sometimes I sit at the table and watch the mixture dribble down her white back. She boils a pot of water on the stove at the same time; when she is finished with her hair, she steams her face. She wants so badly to be beautiful.

I am trying to solve complicated algebraic problems I have set for myself. Since I started cutting school last Friday, the one thing I miss is homework. Find the value for *n*. Will it be a whole number? It is never a whole number. It is always a fraction.

"Will you get me a towel?" my sister asks. She turns her face toward me and clutches her hair to the top of her head. The sprayer hose slithers into its hole next to the faucet.

I hand her a dish towel. "No," she says. "A bath towel. Don't be stupid."

In the bathroom, my mother is watering her plants. She has arranged them in the tub and turned the shower on. She sits on the toilet lid and watches. It smells like outdoors in the bathroom.

I hand my sister the towel and watch her wrap it around her head. She takes the cover off the pot of boiling water and drops lemon slices in. Then she lowers her face into the steam.

This is the problem I have set for myself:

$$\frac{245(n+17)}{34} = 396(n-45)$$

$$n =$$

Wednesday, I stand outside the high-school gym doors. Inside students are lined up doing calisthenics. It's snowing, and prematurely dark, and I can watch without being seen.

"Well," my father says when I get home. He is standing in the garage testing the automatic door. Every time a plane flies overhead, the door opens or closes, so my father is trying to fix it. "Have you changed your mind about school?" he asks me.

I lock my bicycle to a pole. This infuriates my father, who doesn't believe in locking things up in his own house. He pretends not to notice. I wipe the thin stripes of snow off the fenders with my middle finger. It is hard to ride a bike in the snow. This afternoon on my way home from the high school I fell off, and lay in the snowy road with my bike on top of me. It felt warm.

"We're going to get another dog," my father says.

"It's not that," I say. I wish everyone would stop talking about dogs. I can't tell how sad I really am about Keds versus how sad I am in general. If I don't keep these things separate, I feel as if I'm betraying Keds.

"Then what is it?" my father says.

"It's nothing," I say.

My father nods. He is very good about bringing things up and then letting them drop. A lot gets dropped. He presses the button on the automatic control. The door slides down its oiled tracks and falls shut. It's dark in the garage. My father presses the button again and the door opens, and we both look outside at the snow falling in the driveway, as if in those few seconds the world might have changed.

My mother has forgotten to call me for dinner, and when I confront her with this she tells me that she did but that I was sleeping. She is loading the dishwasher. My sister is standing at the counter, listening, and separating eggs for her shampoo.

"What can I get you?" my mother asks. "Would you like a meat-loaf sandwich?"

"No," I say. I open the refrigerator and survey its illuminated contents. "Could I have some eggs?"

"O.K.," my mother says. She comes and stands beside me and puts her hand on top of mine on the door handle. There are no eggs in the refrigerator. "Oh," my mother says; then, "Julie?"

"What?" my sister asks.

"Did you take the last eggs?"

"I guess so," my sister says. "I don't know."

"Forget it," I say. "I won't have eggs."

"No," my mother says. "Julie doesn't need them in her shampoo. That's not what I bought them for."

"I do," my sister says. "It's a formula. It doesn't work without the eggs. I need the protein."

"I don't want eggs," I say. "I don't want anything." I go into my bedroom.

My mother comes in and stands looking out the window. The snow has turned to rain. "You're not the only one who is unhappy about this," she says.

"About what?" I say. I am sitting on my unmade bed. If I pick up my room, my mother will make my bed: that's the deal. I didn't pick up my room this morning.

"About Keds," she says. "I'm unhappy, too. But it doesn't stop me from going to school."

"You don't go to school," I say.

"You know what I mean," my mother says. She turns around and looks at my room, and begins to pick things off the floor.

"Don't do that," I say. "Stop."

My mother drops the dirty clothes in an exaggerated gesture of defeat. She almost—almost—throws them on the floor. The way she holds her hands accentuates their emptiness. "If you're not going to go to school," she says, "the least you can do is clean your room."

In algebra word problems, a boat sails down a river while a jeep drives along the bank. Which will reach the capital first? If a plane flies at a certain speed from Boulder to Oklahoma City and then at a different speed from Oklahoma City to Detroit, how many cups of coffee can the stewardess serve, assuming she is unable to serve during the first and last ten minutes of each flight? How many times can a man ride the elevator to the top of the Empire State Building while his wife climbs the stairs, given that the woman travels one stair slower each flight? And if the man jumps up while the elevator is going down, which is moving—the man, the woman, the elevator, or the snow falling outside?

The next Monday I get up and make preparations for going to school. I can tell at the breakfast table that my mother is afraid to acknowledge them for fear it won't be true. I haven't gotten up before ten o'clock in a week. My mother makes me French toast. I sit at the table and write the note excusing me for my absence. I am eighteen, an adult, and thus able to excuse myself from school. This is what my note says:

Dear Mr. Kelly [my homeroom teacher]:
    Please excuse my absence February 17–24. I was unhappy and did not feel able to attend school.
               Sincerely,
               MICHAEL PECHETTI

This is the exact format my mother used when she wrote my notes, only she always said, "Michael was home with a sore throat," or "Michael was home with a bad cold." The colds that prevented me from going to school were always bad colds.

My mother watches me write the note but doesn't ask to see it. I leave it on the kitchen table when I go to the bathroom, and when I come back to get it I know she has read it. She is washing the bowl she dipped the French toast into. Before, she would let Keds lick it clean. He liked eggs.

*

In Spanish class we are seeing a film on flamenco dancers. The screen wouldn't pull down, so it is being projected on the blackboard, which is green and cloudy with erased chalk. It looks a little like the women are sick, and dancing in Heaven. Suddenly the little phone on the wall buzzes.

Mrs. Smitts, the teacher, gets up to answer it, and then walks over to me. She puts her hand on my shoulder and leans her face close to mine. It is dark in the room. "Miguel," Mrs. Smitts whispers, "*tienes que ir a la oficina de* guidance."

"What?" I say.

She leans closer, and her hair blocks the dancers. Despite the clicking castanets and the roomful of students, there is something intimate about this moment. "*Tienes que ir a la oficina de* guidance," she repeats slowly. Then, "You must go to the guidance office. Now. *Vaya.*"

My guidance counselor, Mrs. Dietrich, used to be a history teacher, but she couldn't take it anymore, so she was moved into guidance. On her immaculate desk is a calendar blotter with "LUNCH" written across the middle of every box, including Saturday and Sunday. The only other things on her desk are an empty photo cube and my letter to Mr. Kelly. I sit down, and she shows me the letter as if I haven't yet read it. I reread it.

"Did you write this?" she asks.

I nod affirmatively. I can tell Mrs. Dietrich is especially nervous about this interview. Our meetings are always charged with tension. At the last one, when I was selecting my second-semester courses, she started to laugh hysterically when I said I wanted to take Boys' Home Ec. Now every time I see her in the halls she stops me and asks how I'm doing in Boys' Home Ec. It's the only course of mine she remembers.

I hand the note back to her and say, "I wrote it this morning," as if this clarifies things.

"This morning?"

"At breakfast," I say.

"Do you think this is an acceptable excuse?" Mrs. Dietrich asks. "For missing more than a week of school?"

"I'm sure it isn't," I say.

"Then why did you write it?"

Because it is the truth, I start to say. It is. But somehow I know that saying this will make me more unhappy. It might make me cry. "I've been doing homework," I say.

"That's fine," Mrs. Dietrich says, "but it's not the point. The point is, to graduate you have to attend school for a hundred and eighty days, or have legitimate excuses for the days you've missed. That's the point. Do you want to graduate?"

"Yes," I say.

"Of course you do," Mrs. Dietrich says.

She crumples my note and tries to throw it into the wastepaper basket but misses. We both look for a second at the note lying on the floor, and then I get up and throw it away. The only other thing in her wastepaper basket is a banana peel. I can picture her eating a banana in her tiny office. This, too, makes me sad.

"Sit down," Mrs. Dietrich says.

I sit down.

"I understand your dog died. Do you want to talk about that?"

"No," I say.

"Is that what you're so unhappy about?" she says. "Or is it something else?"

I almost mention the banana peel in her wastebasket, but I don't. "No," I say. "It's just my dog."

Mrs. Dietrich thinks for a moment. I can tell she is embarrassed to be talking about a dead dog. She would be more comfortable if it were a parent or a sibling.

"I don't want to talk about it," I repeat.

She opens her desk drawer and takes out a pad of hall passes. She begins to write one out for me. She has beautiful handwriting. I think of her learning to write beautifully as a child and then growing up to be a guidance counselor, and this makes me unhappy.

"Mr. Neuman is willing to overlook this matter," she says. Mr. Neuman is the principal. "Of course, you will have to make up all the work you've missed. Can you do that?"

"Yes," I say.

Mrs. Dietrich tears the pass from the pad and hands it to me. Our hands touch. "You'll get over this," she says. "Believe me, you will."

My sister works until midnight at the Photo-Matica. It's a tiny booth in the middle of the A&P parking lot. People drive up and leave their film and come back the next day for the pictures. My sister wears a uniform that makes her look like a counterperson in a fast-food restaurant. Sometimes at night when I'm sick of being at home I walk downtown and sit in the booth with her.

There's a machine in the booth that looks like a printing press, only snapshots ride down a conveyor belt and fall into a bin and then disappear. The machine gives the illusion that your photographs are being developed on the spot. It's a fake. The same fifty photographs roll through over and over, and my sister says nobody notices, because everyone in town is taking the same pictures. She opens up the envelopes and looks at them.

Before I go into the booth, I buy cigarettes in the A&P. It is open twenty-four hours a day, and I love it late at night. It is big and bright and empty. The checkout girl sits on her counter swinging her legs. The Muzak plays "If Ever I Would Leave You." Before I buy the cigarettes, I walk up and down the aisles. Everything looks good to eat, and the things that aren't edible look good in their own way. The detergent aisle is colorful and clean-smelling.

My sister is listening to the radio and polishing her nails when I get to the booth. It is almost time to close.

"I hear you went to school today," she says.

"Yeah."

"How was it?" she asks. She looks at her fingernails, which are so long it's frightening.

"It was O.K.," I say. "We made chili dogs in Home Ec."

"So are you over it all?"

I look at the pictures riding down the conveyor belt. I know the order practically by heart: graduation, graduation, birthday, mountains, baby, baby, new car, bride, bride and groom, house. . . . "I guess so," I say.

"Good," says my sister. "It was getting to be a little much." She puts her tiny brush back in the bottle, capping it. She shows me her nails. They're an odd brown shade. "Cinnamon," she says. "It's an earth color." She looks out into the parking lot. A boy is collecting the abandoned shopping carts, forming a long silver train, which he noses back toward the store. I can tell he is singing by the way his mouth moves.

"That's where we found Keds," my sister says, pointing to the Salvation Army bin.

When I went out to buy cigarettes, Keds would follow me. I hung out down here at night before he died. I was unhappy then, too. That's what no one understands. I named him Keds because he was all white with big black feet and it looked as if he had high-top sneakers on. My mother wanted to name him Bootie. Bootie is a cat's name. It's a dumb name for a dog.

"It's a good thing you weren't here when we found him," my sister says. "You would have gone crazy."

I'm not really listening. It's all nonsense. I'm working on a new problem: Find the value for n such that n plus everything else in your life makes you feel all right. What would n equal? Solve for n.

Chapter 3

Birth/Death

1. The title of this chapter is "Birth/Death."

   a. In your reading log, freewrite for a few minutes about how the words *birth* and *death* are related or not.
   b. Reread what you wrote, and number the different ideas.
   c. Summarize your ideas for a partner.

2. Make two combined lists with your partner: one for the ways in which the words *birth* and *death* are related, and one for the ways in which they are not related.

3. Talk with the class about the relationships you found between the words.

BEFORE READING

1. For everything its season, and for every activity under heaven its time:

   > a time to be born and a time to die;
   > a time to plant and a time to uproot. . . .

   Have you heard or read these words before? Write for a few minutes in your reading log about how these words make you feel.
       Share with a partner some part of what you wrote.

2. Read the poem.

Ecclesiastes 3:1–8

This poem is taken from the Old Testament of the The New English Bible, *a translation that uses present-day English rather than traditional Biblical language.*

For everything its season, and for every activity under heaven its time:

> a time to be born and a time to die;
> a time to plant and a time to uproot;
> a time to kill and a time to heal;
> a time to pull down and a time to build up;
> a time to weep and a time to laugh;
> a time for mourning and a time for dancing;
> a time to scatter stones and a time to gather them;
> a time to embrace and a time to refrain from embracing;
> a time to seek and a time to lose;
> a time to keep and a time to throw away;
> a time to tear and a time to mend;
> a time for silence and a time for speech;
> a time to love and a time to hate;
> a time for war and a time for peace.

AFTER READING

1. With a partner, read the poem aloud, slowly and thoughtfully. If you don't know individual words, try to guess what they mean from the ideas around them.

2. Choose one activity.

Activity A: Read the poem again by yourself, line by line. Stop after each line, and let an image develop in your mind to match the words. In your log, describe some of the images you created, either in words or by drawing a picture. Share what you wrote or drew with your group. See what others did.

Activity B: Freewrite for a few minutes on what you think the essential meaning (or the main point) of this piece is. At the end of your freewriting, summarize the meaning in one kernel sentence. Share your thoughts with the members of your group. Talk about whether you all have similar interpretations of the meaning or different ones.

HOW I READ IT

Think about how the images formed in your mind. Try to describe that process to your group, and find out how other people in the group formed images.

Write a few things in your log that you learned about how you and others in your group read.

HOW IT'S WRITTEN

What makes this piece poetry? Talk about it with your partner, and come up with three or four features. Then, with your partner, add a line to the piece, making your line poetic also.

TOPICS FOR WRITING

Choose one activity.

Activity A: Think of a time when a negative event turned out to have a positive ending. Write about what happened and the outcome. Use as many details as you need to make it clear to the reader. (One of the techniques for gathering ideas, such as clustering, might help you get started. See Appendix A, p. 204.)

Activity B: Pick one of the lines from the poem that has special meaning for you, or add one of your own. Put it at the top of your paper. Write about it, explaining what it means to you.

Activity C: Choose a line from the poem that strikes you as true because of your experience or reading, for example, the line "a time to kill and a time to heal." Explain how the words that are opposites (in this case, *kill* and *heal*) are related, using examples from your experience, observation of others, or reading. The examples may be personal, social, historical, political, or other. In any case, describe the experience or event in as much detail as you can. (One of the techniques for **gathering ideas** might help you recall details. See Appendix A, p. 201.)

AFTER WRITING

1. Read your piece of writing to your group. Ask your group to tell you:
   a. What do they understand your main point is?
   b. What part would they like to hear more about?
   c. What will they remember about your piece?

2. Write in your log about how you wrote this piece. For example, was it easy or hard? Did you write it in one sitting? How did you get your ideas? How did you decide on your main point? How did the poem affect your writing?

BEFORE READING

---

1. As a class, choose one activity.

   Activity A: With your partner, make a list of some things you consider miraculous events. Then put your list into categories and give titles to the categories.

   Talk about these events with your group. Choose the one you like best from the group, and share it with the class.

   Activity B: Is there anything you've witnessed recently that you consider miraculous? Write about it for a few minutes in your journal.

   Read what you wrote to your group. Choose the one you like best from the group, and share it with the class.

2. Read "A Miraculous Event."

A Miraculous Event
Jorge Icaza

Jorge Icaza was a student at Borough of Manhattan Community College/CUNY when he wrote this piece. It appeared in a student publication, ESL Voices.

For all parents, including myself, watching their child being born is one of nature's greatest experiences. I felt very lucky to be present at such a miraculous event.

At first, I thought I wouldn't be able to stand the sight of blood, but for this occasion, courage was very important to me, so I made that decision. After all, it is just a simple fact of nature that we all have gone through.

I can still remember the way the doctor was leading the childbirth. I still remember how my wife reacted to the contractions and her effort to do so. I felt as if I was a video camera and couldn't take my eyes off her.

Suddenly, the doctor asked me to get closer. There it was, the head of the baby starting to come out. They never thought that the baby would be so big, so they had to cut a little on the vagina. Then, another contraction came and the head was out.

While pulling the arms, they were getting ready to catch the baby. Then, the last contraction came and that was it. A little girl was born.

It took only forty-five minutes for her to be born. After they cleaned up my newborn daughter, I held her in my arms and then showed her to my wife.

My wife thought I was disappointed because I wanted a boy instead. But after I had watched all of the pain and effort that she had made, how could I be disappointed?

I just gave thanks to God for the beautiful gift that he gave me.

AFTER READING

1. In your reading log, write for a few minutes:

   What were the father's thoughts and feelings as he witnessed the birth of his daughter?

   What were your thoughts and feelings as you read this piece?

   Read what you wrote to your group.

2. The father says that his wife thinks he is disappointed over the birth of a girl instead of a boy. He says he is not disappointed. What do you think the issue is here? Discuss this with your group. State the issue, and write two or three questions about it. (See p. 32 for a discussion of issues.) Put your questions on the chalkboard for the class to see.

HOW IT'S WRITTEN

1. Reread the piece, and underline all the words that evoke emotions. Put + for positive emotions and – for negative ones. Notice who was feeling the emotion. Work with a partner if you'd like.

2. Find the sentence that you think best expresses the main point of the piece. See if others in your group agree with you. If not, choose one sentence you agree on. Then circle all the words or phrases in the rest of the piece that support that idea. Do you find any words or phrases that don't support it?

3. In your log, write about what you learned from looking at how "A Miraculous Event" was written that you could apply to your own writing.

TOPICS FOR WRITING

Choose one activity.

Activity A: The father said he felt like he was a video camera watching his daughter's birth; he couldn't take his eyes off his wife. Sit in a public place where you can imagine you are a video camera, and write the story that takes place in front of you.

Activity B: Pick a miraculous event you have witnessed or experienced. (Look back at Before Reading, Activity A or B.) Tell what happened just as this writer has done. As you write, pretend that you are a video camera. That may help you see specific details.

Activity C: The father said his wife thought that he was disappointed, that he wanted a boy instead of a girl. He said he wasn't. Why would the wife think this? What's the difference between having a boy or a girl baby in a family? How do you feel about this issue? How does your culture view it? Look back at the questions in After Reading 2. Choosing one of them may focus your thoughts.

AFTER WRITING

1. Form a group with others who wrote on the same topic. Read your paper aloud to the group. Ask your group to tell you:
   a. What they like best about your writing
   b. What the focus of your writing is
   c. One suggestion they have for improving the focus—can it be sharpened or made clearer?
2. Write in your log about how your group members reacted to your paper.

BEFORE READING

1. Read the introductory information. What words come to your mind when you think of the birth of a younger brother or sister? Brainstorm for a few minutes with your group, and come up with a list.

2. Read the story.

Birthing
Kate Simon

This excerpt is from Bronx Primitive: Portraits in a Childhood, *Kate Simon's autobiography of growing up in an immigrant neighborhood in the Bronx, New York, in the 1920s. It tells about the time her mother gave birth to a third child and how 8-year-old Kate, the oldest child, felt and behaved toward her mother, the baby, and her younger brother.*

When school started in September before I was quite eight, the walks with my swollen mother—watching her skirt so that she didn't stumble on the stairs, pacing my steps, skipping in place to her lumbering, rocking walk, like the elephant in the zoo—stopped. When we came home from school there was a quiet in the house that seemed to tremble against the walls, no lilting greetings, no apples and crackers on the table, in the sink a cold half cup of tea with milk. She was resting, and resting meant sick, like the times when Dr. James had come and gone. It also meant trouble. I kept glancing surreptitiously at her ankles to see if they were swollen. In scraps of eavesdropping I had accumulated something about women swelling and having convulsions before babies were born. My mother had swelled but didn't have convulsions when I was born, a difficult delivery, "with instruments" that dented my forehead. . . .

"Instruments" were enormous black pincers, like those the iceman used to pull blocks of ice from his wagon, stuck in my mother's belly, ripping through the flesh and searching among her bleeding bowels until it hit my forehead and grabbed me, pulling up and out again through the red, messed flesh into the air, and dropped me, a doll covered with pee and shit, into hands that slapped to make me breathe. And now, in our house, a few paces from the kitchen, fewer from the dining room, it was probably all going to happen again; tonight, tomorrow night, the next night. It always happened late at night, a shameful, secret thing, too dark and terrible for open day.

One afternoon in early October we came home to find Mrs. Nagy and Mrs. Kaplan bustling around the kitchen and Fannie Herman standing in the hallway wringing her hands. Mrs. Nagy gave us a piece of strudel and told us brusquely to go down and stay in the street until our father came home. We hung around the stoop feeling uncomfortable, lost. We had to go to the toilet, we were getting cold in the falling light, we didn't feel like playing. Something was happening to our mother and why couldn't we see her? It had to do with her belly and the baby. I wanted to watch and at the same time wanted to be far, far away; to be someone else in another place, a girl who lived in a book. . . .

During the night we were awakened by a shriek and then another. Our door was pushed shut and we knew we were not to open it, not to get out of bed, not to see what was happening. People bustled in the hallway, to and from the kitchen, to and from the bathroom. Someone rang the doorbell and was admitted, probably the doctor. Through the sound of feet and the hushed voices, another scream and more, louder, more piercing, like ambulances. This I, too, had done to my mother, distorted her good-natured, singing person into a howling animal. I imagined her hair wild and swept across her staring green eyes, her pretty mouth torn by the screams, the doctor pushing the immense pincers into her belly and searching, searching for the baby, ripping her to pieces as my birth had done. My brother was asleep or pretended to be. I was alone in a guilt that made me want to disappear, to die.

Not knowing how to die, I separated myself from myself, one girl not there, one girl going through familiar actions in a dumbness and deafness like a thick rubber Halloween mask. I don't know who gave us breakfast; I ate it. I don't know what happened in school; I was there and managed to perform whatever was asked of me. I did my homework; it was correct. They told me I had a little sister; I didn't say anything. The women on the street asked me how my mother was; I said all right. This went on, the living in a cold, flat country, for several days, the guilt pushed down, out, away, and kept away. When my mother called to me from her bedroom to come and see the new baby, it was pretty, I called back, "Tomorrow," and ran to the street.

One of the days when my mother was still in her bed and we still fed by the neighbors, a monitor came into my classroom and handed a note to the teacher. . . . My teacher called me to her and told me that I was wanted by my brother's teacher. All the kids stared as I walked awkwardly (was my skirt hitched up in back? my socks falling?) out of the room. When I reached his classroom, my brother was standing at her desk, looking shamefaced but not especially stricken. His teacher, Miss Sullivan, one of the smiling young ones, said she knew my mother had just had a baby but a big girl like myself could take care of a little brother almost as well as his mother could. But maybe I was too busy to notice that he didn't wash too well. Pulling his collar away from his neck, she showed me a broad band of dirt that began at a sharp edge just below his clean jaws. I had said every morning, "Wash your face," but forgot to mention his neck. Everything became hard and clear, as if it were cut out of metal, in that room, . . .: Miss Sullivan's blond lashes, her left eye a little bigger than the right, the spot of spit at the corner of her dry lips, the gray clouds of old chalk marks on the blackboard, the word cards, SENT, WENT, BENT, on the wall, the gluey tan wood of the windowsill, the pale afternoon sun streaking the floor, a red sweater and a brown sweater hanging crooked in the half-open wardrobe, the brown desks on iron legs . . .

I stood there leaden with shame until Miss Sullivan dismissed me with, "See that he washes better," and sent me back to my classroom. It was difficult to open the door and walk into those eyes that were going to stare at me and later, at three o'clock, come closer to ask what happened. I answered, "Oh, nothing. Miss Sullivan wanted me to check my brother's homework; he's careless, she said." I wanted to vomit, to stamp, to scream, to break, to kill: him, me, them, my mother, my father, everything, the whole world. But I had to walk him home. He searched my face as he ran across the playground toward me, hesitated, and attached himself to Jimmy, walking near me, as he had to, but a safe distance away, on the far side of Jimmy. As soon as he dropped his books on the floor of our bedroom he ran into my mother's room, where I heard them giggling together. She called to me, "Don't you want to come and see the baby?" I yelled back, "Tomorrow," still afraid of what I might see, a baby with a ditch in its head, a mother all rags of flesh, an exploded, splashed cartoon animal. All my fault. My brother came back into the kitchen where I was trying to peel an apple in one long coil, an especially delicate operation because I was using a big breadknife. He pushed my arm, breaking the coil, and ran toward the hallway, laughing. I threw the knife at him and saw it quivering in the wall where his head had been a second before. It fell from the wall. I picked it up and continued cutting the apple as I listened to him screaming to my mother, "She tried to kill me! She threw the knife, the big knife, at me! She's crazy! Send her away! Please, Mama, send her away! I'm afraid of her!" I heard her slippers patter down the hall, closed my eyes tight shut, and waited. She shook me. "Open your eyes. Look at me." I looked, I would have to sometime, and saw her as she was most mornings, in her thick brown bathrobe, her short hair not yet combed, her lips pale. "What's the matter with you? Do you know you could have killed him? Do you know that he would be dead, forever dead? Never talk again, never walk, never see, never hear? Do you know that you would be locked away in an asylum for crazy people? And spend the rest of your life, many, many years, with other crazies?" I said nothing, tried not to be there. "I've got to go back to bed now and attend to the baby. This your father will hear about and I won't get in his way. Whatever punishment you get you'll deserve.". . .

By the time my brother and father got home and the wet umbrella placed in the bathtub, the story of the knife had been told, so serious a matter that it came before supper. Asked why I had thrown the knife, I answered—and it seemed a feeble reason— "Because his neck was dirty and he made me ashamed in front of his whole class." I couldn't say, "Because I hate mothers and babies and screaming in the night and people being pulled out of bellies with instruments and brothers who jump around and play while I have to take care of them." I couldn't find the words or shape the sentence because they were truly crazy things to say, worse than throwing knives. There was no preliminary lecture, cause and effect clear and simple. With a few words to my mother . . . my father pushed me into the bathroom and, while he carefully pulled his belt out of the trouser loops, told me to lie across the covered toilet, pick up my skirt, and pull down my bloomers. . . . There was no preparation for the pain beyond pain of this first beating, the swish of the strap becoming a burning scream through my whole body, my arms shaking as they clung to the edge of the bathtub, my fingers scratching at the squealing porcelain, my ribs crushed against the toilet lid. I shrieked and begged, "Papa, don't. Stop, please. Please stop. Please, Papa." He stopped when he was out of breath, his face red, his brown eyes bulging. Replacing his belt, he walked out of the bathroom, closing the door. I stood there for a long while, then splashed cold water on my behind, fixed my clothing, and stood some more, not knowing where to go. In time I heard fumbling at the doorknob and my mother's voice telling my brother to get away, to let me be. A few minutes later she opened the door to tell me it was time to eat. I slipped out of the bathroom and into my bedroom, pushed the big chair against the door that had no lock, piled my books, my brother's books, the wooden sewing machine cover, and the heavy coats that were in the closet on the chair, and got into bed, pushing myself way, way down under the featherbed, stroking and rubbing myself until I fell asleep.

The next morning my brother banged on the door for his books. As I pulled the heavy chair away so he could get in, I noticed his neck was clean. My mother was back in bed with the baby I had no intention of seeing. I grabbed a roll from the breadbox in the kitchen and ate it as I dressed, then left the house quickly, passing my brother, who stood on the third floor waiting at Jimmy's door. We avoided each other for the next day or two, he hanging on to Jimmy, I watching that they looked each way down the street before they crossed broad, busy 180th.

After my mother had spent her traditional ten days in bed, she put on the clothing she wore before the big belly and fixed us nice lunches: noodles, pot cheese, and raisins with cinnamon and sugar, radishes and cucumbers in sour cream, salami sandwiches. Ordinariness washed, day by day, over our lives except for the baby lying in my mother's lap in the kitchen. She looked unfinished and wandering, making strange faces, her eyes a milky blue and bobbling in her head, the tiny fingers reaching and curling toward everything, nothing. When her eyes turned to gold and steady, and some of the grimaces became smiles, I began to like her a little and let her pull at my fingers and hair.

AFTER READING

1. With your group, talk about what you understand the story to be about. Next, read the story again, looking for confirmation and support for your understanding. Talk again with your group. Then write a short summary of the story.

2. Look through the story, and mark the positive (+) and negative (−) emotions felt by the young girl. Work with a partner if you'd like.

   List the emotions in your reading log. Are there some opposing pairs, like *love-hate*? Put them together. Share your list with your group.

HOW IT'S WRITTEN

1. With a partner, choose one activity.

   Activity A: Nowhere does the writer directly say that the child is jealous of the birth of the new baby. Find a paragraph where the writer shows jealousy but does not tell it.

   Activity B: Read the section beginning "I stood there" to the end of the paragraph. What various emotions do you think the little girl is showing, even though she only names (or tells) one, *shame*? Make a list. Be able to point to something in the text that supports each item on your list.

2. Do you understand the difference between *showing* and *telling* in writing? With your partner, select an example from the reading where the author is showing, not telling an emotion. Tell the class what you think the difference is, and show them your example.

TOPICS FOR WRITING

Choose one activity.

Activity A: Choose three or four lines from the reading from Ecclesiastes (p. 78) that relate to this story. Explain them in a way that might help the older child in the story.

Activity B: Write a letter to an 8-year-old child (the one in the story or another child you know or imagine) in a similar state of mind. You want to help the child feel better about the birth of a baby in the family. Share your experience with the arrival of a new sibling, offer sympathy, a lesson to be learned, comfort, or advice. Remember, the child is only 8.

Activity C: Look back over your notes and lists, and pick one of the emotions the 8-year-old felt, perhaps anger or jealousy. Tell an experience from your past in which you suffered the same feeling. As you write about it, try to *show* the emotion by giving details of how you looked, behaved, talked, and acted.

AFTER WRITING

1. Read your piece of writing aloud to one person in your group. Before you read, tell who you wrote the piece for. For example, did you write it to a child, or were you thinking of someone else? Ask the listener to write you a response:
   a. Where did you *show* instead of *tell*?
   b. What could you add, and where, to *show* more?
2. If you wish, add to your writing based on your partner's comments.
3. Read your writing aloud to the whole group. As a group, choose one piece to read aloud to the whole class.
4. Write in your log on what you learned about writing from reading "Birthing" and writing your own composition. Share this with the whole class.

BEFORE READING

1. Write down two or three words that come to your mind when you think of the word *mirrors*.

   Combine your list of words with your partner's. Be sure you have at least five different words. (Save this list.)

2. Read the introductory information. What do you suppose the title, "Mirrors," means in that context? Write your thoughts in your reading log.

   Share your thoughts with your partner.

3. Read the short excerpt.

Mirrors
Susan Kenney

This excerpt is taken from a chapter of In Another Country *in which the writer tells of some childhood memories of her father, who died when she was 12.*

My father died suddenly when he was forty and I was twelve. For years after his death I was bitterly resentful of his abrupt departure: I tried to keep the memory of him, his voice, his face, the color of his hair, the way he moved, the clothes he wore, and noted the anniversary of his death each year as it came around. Five years, ten years, twelve, and he had been dead as long as I knew him; fifteen, twenty-five, the years passing so quickly that soon he would be dead as long as he had been alive. I regarded that anniversary with an almost physical dread; we are alive so little and dead so long, and even in the memories of those who want to keep us we fade away.

AFTER READING

1. Write in your log:

   What do you understand or see in what you just read?

   How do you feel about what you understand or see?

   What do you associate with your understanding?

2. List the words you and your partner compiled in Before Reading 1 across the top of your paper as headings. Put the following words under the headings you think they go with, for any reason. You can put one word under several headings if you see a connection or if you and you partner don't agree. Explain to your partner the connections you make and why you put a word where you put it.

color	resentful
voice	fade away
anniversary	abrupt
dread	memories

3. Talk with your group about any connections you now see between this passage and the title, "Mirrors." You might see something you didn't see before.

TOPICS FOR WRITING

Choose one activity.

Activity A: Pick a sentence or phrase from the passage that is moving or powerful to you. Use it as the starting point for something you write: a short essay, a story, a memory, a poem, a letter.

Activity B: You may hear someone describe a person as the "image" of the father or mother. That means the person looks or acts just like one of the parents. What about you? Are you a reflection of one of your parents? Which one? One more than the other? Or both? How? Write a composition about yourself as a reflection.

Activity C: Find a photograph of a person from your past who is no longer in your life. Write about that person. Tell the story of the photograph, where it was taken, what was going on, who took it. Put the photograph into words, describing the person you see, face, color of hair, voice, the way the person moved, and feelings you associate with the picture.

AFTER WRITING

1. Give your piece a title. Think about the connection between the title and the piece.

2. Read your writing aloud to your group. Ask the group to jot down what they remember of your writing. Ask them to tell you what they wrote down. Did they understand what you meant to say? (You don't have to respond to them; just listen.)

3. Ask the group what words from your piece connect with your title.

4. Write in your log about how you wrote this piece. Was it easy or hard? How did you get your ideas? What did you learn?

BEFORE READING

1. What words come to your mind when you hear the word *mother?* Write them down. Then share them with your partner. Put your combined list on the chalkboard.

2. This story is a reminiscence about the narrator's mother. The memories told in the story were triggered by a song. Write for a few minutes about songs that remind you of special people or events in your life. (If the song is in another language, translate the title.)
Share what you wrote with your partner.

3. Read the story "Mother."

Mother
Grace Paley

Grace Paley is a novelist and short-story writer who has lived in New York City. She often writes about relationships between parents and children, husbands and wives, friends and strangers.

One day I was listening to the AM radio. I heard a song: "Oh, I Long to See My Mother in the Doorway." By God! I said, I understand that song. I have often longed to see my mother in the doorway. As a matter of fact, she did stand frequently in various doorways looking at me. She stood one day, just so, at the front door, the darkness of the hallway behind her. It was New Year's Day. She said sadly, If you come home at 4 A.M. when you're seventeen, what time will you come home when you're twenty? She asked this question without humor or meanness. She had begun her worried preparations for death. She would not be present, she thought, when I was twenty. So she wondered.

Another time she stood in the doorway of my room. I had just issued a political manifesto attacking the family's position on the Soviet Union. She said, Go to sleep for godsakes, you damn fool, you and your Communist ideas. We saw them already, Papa and me, in 1905. We guessed it all.

At the door of the kitchen she said, You never finish your lunch. You run around senselessly. What will become of you?

Then she died.

Naturally for the rest of my life I longed to see her, not only in doorways, in a great number of places—in the dining room with my aunts, at the window looking up and down the block, in the country garden among zinnias and marigolds, in the living room with my father.

They sat in comfortable leather chairs. They were listening to Mozart. They looked at one another amazed. It seemed to them that they'd just come over on the boat. They'd just learned the first English words. It seemed to them that he had just proudly handed in a 100 percent correct exam to the American anatomy professor. It seemed as though she'd just quit the shop for the kitchen.

I wish I could see her in the doorway of the living room.

She stood there a minute. Then she sat beside him. They owned an expensive record player. They were listening to Bach. She said to him, Talk to me a little. We don't talk so much anymore.

I'm tired, he said. Can't you see? I saw maybe thirty people today. All sick, all talk talk talk talk. Listen to the music, he said. I believe you once had perfect pitch. I'm tired, he said.

Then she died.

AFTER READING

1. After you've read the piece, write an entry in your reading log. Write about what you understand in the text and how you feel about it. Save this entry.

2. With your partner, choose one activity. Then share it with your group.

   Activity A: With your partner, list the events in *chronological* order. How much time is covered in the story? Why did the writer put the events in the order she did?

   Compare your list to others' lists in your group. Do you have the same order? Put the group list on the board, and have one person from the group explain it to the class.

   Activity B: The mother says to the narrator, "You and your Communist ideas. We saw them already, Papa and me, in 1905." What do you understand by her words? What background information can you provide about events in the Soviet Union in 1905 to add to the meaning of the story?

Work with your partner on this. You may need to go to the library to look in an encyclopedia or history book. Share your information with the class.

HOW I READ IT

1. Talk with your group about how you came to understand the story. How many times did you read it? Did you understand it right away? Did you understand it better after writing in your log about it? After talking?

2. Write in your reading log several things you learned from talking with others that might help you read better.

HOW IT'S WRITTEN

1. With a partner, choose one activity.

   Activity A: The author repeated the sentence "Then she died." Why did the author do that? What is the significance of repeating the sentence?

   Talk about these questions with your partner, and come up with an answer that satisfies you both. Write about your answer in your reading log.

   Activity B: A *motif* is an element, image, or concept that is repeated throughout a piece of writing or any creative work. One of the motifs in this story is music. Circle every reference to music. Find another motif. Underline every reference to it.

   Talk with your partner about why the writer chose these particular motifs. What purpose do they serve? When you have an answer that satisfies you, write a paragraph about it in your reading log.

   Activity C: With your partner, look back through the story, and mark all the instances where the writer names things, for example, where instead of using a general word like *flower*, she uses the name of the flower, *zinnia*. Substitute a general word where she gives the name to see what difference it makes. Talk with your partner about the effect of using such specific details as the names of things.

2. Share what you and your partner found with the whole class. Talk about the function of repetition and motifs in this story.

TOPICS FOR WRITING

Choose one activity.

Activity A: Write a reminiscence of someone who was close to you and left you or died. Recall some familiar places and events you associate with that person. Choose several of those memories that seem to be related. (Use one of the techniques for gathering ideas, such as **clustering**, to help you recall details. See Appendix A, p. 204.) You may follow the pattern of the story, using a motif and repetition.

Activity B: In both "Mirrors" and "Mother," the narrators recall the voices of their parents or grandparents, sometimes even specific words. Can you recall something your parent or grandparent told you many years ago? Tell the story about the quotation you remember.

Activity C: In this story, the narrator's parents came to the United States from the Soviet Union. Like many immigrants, they learned English, worked hard, and raised a child. The child, however, grew up with different political views and behaved in ways that upset her mother, like staying out late and eating fast. What generalizations can you make about the children of immigrant parents, who are born in the new country or come when they are very young? About their behavior? Their relationship with their parents? Choose one generalization, and support it from your own experience, this story or other pieces from this book, and your observations of others.

AFTER WRITING

1. Read your piece aloud to your group. Ask the group members to tell you what they like about your piece. Ask them to write down something they noticed about your writing.

2. Read their comments.

3. Write in your log about how you wrote this. For example, how did you choose your topic? Did you use freewriting or clustering or

another technique to get ideas or remember details? Did you try to remember names of things? How did you decide what to start with? How did you determine what order to put things in? Did you get any ideas from the story "Mother"?

4. Share what you wrote in your log with your group.

1. Read the title of the story and the introductory information. In your log, write down what you expect one or two of the author's feelings, thoughts, or reactions to be. Share your thoughts with a partner.
2. Read the excerpt "Father."

Father
Yasushi Inouye

In this excerpt from Chronicle of My Mother, *Yasushi Inouye writes about the impact of his father's death. His father was 80 years old when he died. Inouye, a middle-aged adult at the time, had not been especially close to his father, but he had some surprising feelings and reactions after his father died.*

When Father was seventy he had a cancer, which was successfully removed by surgery. Ten years later, however, the malignancy recurred and he was confined to bed for half a year while his condition gradually deteriorated. Because of his age, surgery was not considered, and death became just a matter of time. Toward the end, for almost a month, we expected each day to be his last. My sisters, brother, and I brought our funeral clothes home and commuted between Tokyo and the village, waiting for the invalid's death. The last time I visited Father the doctor told me he would probably hold out for four or five more days, so I returned that night to Tokyo. But the next day, during my absence, Father drew his last breath. He was clearheaded to the very end, giving detailed instructions to those around him about what meals to prepare for people who visited him and whom to notify of his death.

The last time I saw him, when I informed him that I was going to Tokyo but would return in two or three days, he took his emaciated right hand out from beneath the bed clothes and reached toward me. Since Father had never done anything like that before, I could not understand what he wanted, but I took his hand in mine. Then Father clasped it. Just that—two hands gently holding onto each other. Then in the next instant I felt my hand being softly pushed away. It was a sensation similar to the slight jerk of the tip of a fishing rod. I was startled and withdrew my hand quickly. I still don't know how to interpret this, but I had the distinct feeling that Father was expressing some deep, inner reaction by this gesture, and at that moment I felt chilled, chastised—as if Father were saying, "You're being arrogant, holding your father's hand. It's no joke," and suddenly I felt rejected.

For some time after Father's death this incident stayed in my mind, and I speculated about it like one obsessed. Perhaps, realizing he was near death, Father had stretched out his hand to express his love for me for the last time as a father and then, suddenly despising such feelings in himself, had pushed my hand away. This seemed to be the most plausible explanation. But perhaps it was not so. Perhaps Father had sensed something amiss in my response, and thus had immediately withdrawn the love he was trying to express and let go of my hand. . . .

Yet, on the other hand, I could not rid myself of a nagging doubt. Perhaps I was the one who had pushed away his hand, just as I had thought it possible that he had let go of my hand. . . . I was deeply distressed whenever this possibility intruded on my thoughts.

Finally, I was released from endless musing over this small, last incident between us. It happened quite suddenly and unexpectedly. One day it occurred to me that in his grave Father, like me, might be pondering the meaning of that secret, barely perceptible interchange. Suddenly I felt free. With this fantasy I felt like my father's child for the first time, something that had never happened during his lifetime. I knew: I am my father's child, and he is my father.

After Father's death, I was frequently struck by my resemblance to him in many ways. While he was alive the thought never occurred to me, assured as I was by those around me that I had a totally different personality. From the time I was a student I consciously willed myself not to think like Father, not to behave like him, although it would have been hard to find any similarity between us. Father was a misanthrope from his youth, whereas I always had many friends, was an athlete during my student days, and genuinely liked to be in the center of things. This gregariousness stayed with me after I left university and entered the real world, and when I myself reached the age at which Father had retired I did not consider the possibility of withdrawing to the village and shutting myself away. After my mid-forties I left the newspaper company I was working in to make a fresh start as a writer, the same age Father had cut off all connections with society.

Yet after Father died I would feel him inside me at odd moments. Sometimes when stepping off the veranda into the garden, for example, or groping for my garden slippers, I would feel that I had taken on the same mannerisms as Father. I had similar feelings when I spread out the newspapers in the living room and bent over to read them. There were times when I would pick up a pack of cigarettes, become aware that I was going through some of the same gestures as Father, and unconsciously set the pack down. In the morning, looking into the bathroom mirror while shaving—rinsing the brush and squeezing the water from it—I would realize, "You are doing exactly what Father did."

Quite apart from the mannerisms, it dawned on me that I might be slipping into Father's way of thinking. When working I frequently get up from my desk to sit on a wicker chair on the veranda, letting my thoughts wander at random, with no connection to the work at hand. At those times I always fix my gaze on the old Chinese ash tree, which has branches spreading out in all directions. One day I recalled that Father also looked out at the branches of a tree as he sat in his wicker chair on the veranda in our country home. I felt then as if I were staring into a deep pool in front of me. I was overawed by the realization that Father had lost himself in thought in the same way. With feelings like these, the image of Father as a distinct and individual human being formed in my mind. I began to see him and talk with him frequently.

I also became aware that one of the roles Father performed in his lifetime was to shield me from death. While he was alive I had the feeling—this was not conscious, it lay somewhere in the back of my mind—that I need not think of my own mortality. But after Father passed away that region lying between myself and death came more into focus; the view was no longer totally obstructed and, like it or not, I had to look at one part of the sea of death. I began to think that my turn would come. Thus I came to realize, only after Father died, that by the mere fact of his living, a father protects his child. This was not something that Father was aware of either; it is simply part of the parent-child relationship, yet it is undoubtedly as elemental as any parental bond.

After Father's death, I started envisaging my own death as an incident perhaps not too far off. However, since Mother was still healthy, the sea of death was half-screened from me, and very different from what it is today.

AFTER READING

1. Freewrite in your reading log about your feelings and thoughts as you read this piece. Share some of your freewriting with a partner.

2. With your partner, look back at what you wrote in Before Reading, what you expected Inouye's feelings, thoughts, and reactions would be. Then look through the passage and find other feelings and reactions he had that you didn't expect. Write those down in your log.

3. Go through the passage and mark things that are similar to your own experience and feelings with a plus (+) and things that are different with a minus (−). Share what you find with your partner.

HOW IT'S WRITTEN

With your group, find two or three examples of places where Inouye *shows* through examples and details the thoughts or feelings he has about his father. For example, how does he show that he was struck by his resemblance to his father? Find the sentence that *tells* and the part that *shows*.

Share your findings with the class. As a class, you may want to look back at "Birthing" to compare how two writers *show* meaning.

TOPICS FOR WRITING

Choose one activity.

Activity A: Choose a sentence from the story that you find moving or powerful. Use it as the beginning of an autobiographical piece, an opinion essay, a story, a poem, a letter, or thoughts.

Activity B: Inouye writes, "From the time I was a student I consciously willed myself not to think like Father, not to behave like him." Why do you think he did that? Do you think it often happens that a child tries to be different from a parent? Why do children do this? What has your experience been? And what was the outcome? Write about how you feel about this behavior and your experiences and observations.

Activity C: This excerpt contains feelings and reactions that people often have when a parent dies. People may be surprised by these thoughts and feelings and wonder if it is "normal" to feel this way. It is comforting to know that other people have similar thoughts and emotions. Write an essay in the form of an open letter to an adult whose parent has died. Comfort the person and tell what feelings to expect in the days to come. Use your own experience and examples from the readings "Father," "Mirrors," and "Mother" to support (show) what you mean.

AFTER WRITING

1. Exchange papers with another person in your group. Read the person's paper, and respond in writing, telling what you understand the person is saying and the feelings you think the person is expressing. Lightly with a pencil, put a plus (+) in the margin wherever the person *shows* instead of *tells*.

2. Read the response to your own writing. Based on the feedback, decide if your writing *shows* what you mean. Do you think you should add anything to it? If so, what? Add it if you wish.

3. Now read all the papers in your group. Together, choose one to read to the whole class.

BEFORE READING

1. Read the title of the article and the introductory information. What do you think the title means? Talk about it with the class.

2. Skim the article by reading *only* the first sentence of each paragraph. Read the first sentence (there are 11), and think about them. Write for a few minutes in your reading log about what meaning you get from skimming.

3. Read the first three paragraphs. Stop for a moment and think. Then go back and reread. Don't worry about the meanings of particular words you don't understand. Try to get the essence of what Thomas is saying.

4. Summarize for yourself what he has said so far.

5. Read the whole article.

Death in the Open
Lewis Thomas

Lewis Thomas is a writer and a doctor. This selection is taken from his book The Lives of a Cell: Notes of a Biology Watcher.

Most of the dead animals you see on highways near the cities are dogs, a few cats. Out in the countryside, the forms and coloring of the dead are strange; these are the wild creatures. Seen from a car window they appear as fragments, evoking memories of woodchucks, badgers, skunks, voles, snakes, sometimes the mysterious wreckage of a deer.

It is always a queer shock, part a sudden upwelling of grief, part unaccountable amazement. It is simply astounding to see an animal dead on a highway. The outrage is more than just the location; it is the impropriety of such visible death, anywhere. You do not expect to see dead animals in the open. It is the nature of animals to die alone, off somewhere, hidden. It is wrong to see them lying out on the highway; it is wrong to see them anywhere.

Everything in the world dies, but we only know about it as a kind of abstraction. If you stand in a meadow, at the edge of a hillside, and look around carefully, almost everything you can catch sight of is in the process of dying, and most things will be dead long before you are. If it were not for the constant renewal and replacement going on before your eyes, the whole place would turn to stone and sand under your feet.

There are some creatures that do not seem to die at all; they simply vanish totally into their own progeny. Single cells do this. The cell becomes two, then four, and so on, and after a while the last trace is gone. It cannot be seen as death; barring mutation, the descendants are simply the first cell, living all over again. The cycles of the slime mold have episodes that seem as conclusive as death, but the withered slug, with its stalk and fruiting body, is plainly the transient tissue of a developing animal; the free-swimming amebocytes use this organ collectively in order to produce more of themselves.

There are said to be a billion billion insects on the earth at any moment, most of them with very short life expectancies by our standards. Someone has estimated that there are 25 million assorted insects hanging in the air over every temperate square mile, in a column extending upward for thousands of feet, drifting through the layers of the atmosphere like plankton. They are dying steadily, some by being eaten, some just dropping in their tracks, tons of them around the earth, disintegrating as they die, invisibly.

Who ever sees dead birds, in anything like the huge numbers stipulated by the certainty of the death of all birds? A dead bird is an incongruity, more startling than an unexpected live bird, sure evidence to the human mind that something has gone wrong. Birds do their dying off somewhere, behind things, under things, never on the wing.

Animals seem to have an instinct for performing death alone, hidden. Even the largest, most conspicuous ones find ways to conceal themselves in time. If an elephant missteps and dies in an open place, the herd will not leave him there; the others will pick him up and carry the body from place to place, finally putting it down in some inexplicably suitable location. When elephants encounter the skeleton of an elephant out in the open, they methodically take up each of the bones and distribute them, in a ponderous ceremony, over neighboring acres.

It is a natural marvel. All of the life of the earth dies, all of the time, in the same volume as the new life that dazzles us each morning, each spring. All we see of this is the odd stump, the fly struggling on the porch floor of the summer house in October, the fragment on the highway. I have lived all my life with an embarrassment of squirrels in my backyard, they are all over the place, all year long, and I have never seen, anywhere, a dead squirrel.

I suppose it is just as well. If the earth were otherwise, and all the dying were done in the open, with the dead there to be looked at, we would never have it out of our minds. We can forget about it much of the time, or think of it as an accident to be avoided, somehow. But it does make the process of dying seem more exceptional than it really is, and harder to engage in at the times when we must ourselves engage.

In our way, we conform as best we can to the rest of nature. The obituary pages tell us of the news that we are dying away, while the birth announcements in finer print, off at the side of the page, inform us of our replacements, but we get no grasp from this of the enormity of scale. There are 3 billion of us on the earth, and all 3 billion must be dead, on a schedule, within this lifetime. The vast mortality, involving something over 50 million of us each year, takes place in relative secrecy. We can only really know of the deaths in our households, or among our friends. These, detached in our minds from all the rest, we take to be unnatural events, anomalies, outrages. We speak of our own dead in low voices; struck down, we say, as though visible death can only occur for cause, by disease or violence, avoidably. We send off for flowers, grieve, make ceremonies, scatter bones, unaware of the rest of the 3 billion on the same schedule. All of that immense mass of flesh and bone and consciousness will disappear by absorption into the earth, without recognition by the transient survivors.

Less than a half century from now, our replacements will have more than doubled the numbers. It is hard to see how we can continue to keep the secret, with such multitudes doing the dying. We will have to give up the notion that death is catastrophe, or detestable, or avoidable, or even strange. We will need to learn more about the cycling of life in the rest of the system, and about our connection to the process. Everything that comes alive seems to be in trade for something that dies, cell for cell. There might be some comfort in the recognition of synchrony, in the formation that we all go down together, in the best of company.

AFTER READING

1. With a partner, underline the ideas that strike you as important. Talk about them with your partner. Then present them to your group, and see if others agree that they are the important ones.

2. With your group, find a sentence in the article that you think best expresses the main point or idea. Then write a summary that includes the important ideas. You can write a group summary, or you can each write one, then compare your versions later, and select the best one.

   Share your group summary with the class.

HOW I READ IT

1. In your reading log, write for a few minutes about the following:
   a. Did talking about the title before reading help you to read? How?
   b. Did skimming the article beforehand affect your reading? How?
   c. Did stopping after reading three paragraphs help your understanding or not? How and why or why not?

2. After you have written for a few minutes, share your answers with your group. Make a list of ways that group members read similarly or differently.
   Report to the whole class.

TOPICS FOR WRITING

Choose one activity.

Activity A: "Everything that comes alive seems to be in trade for something that dies, cell for cell." Think of this sentence in terms of ideas, cultures, inventions, species, or nations. (To get started, make a list or a cluster and then talk with a partner.) Write about the relationship between the sentence and one subject you know about from your background, reading, or other courses. Be as specific as you can, giving names and details.

Activity B: Death in the open for an animal or a human is uncommon. The writer suggests that because death is usually hidden, we make more of it than we should. Do you know a place in the world where death is not as hidden as it is in the United States? Write about the place and how death is treated there, explaining it to us.

Activity C: In the United States, parents often try to hide death from children. What do you think about that? Do you think children should be protected from knowing about death? Why? How long? What have you experienced or observed or read that supports your opinion?

AFTER WRITING

1. Exchange your paper with two other people in your group. Read each of their papers several times. Think about what the person is

saying or trying to say. If you wish, mark some of the key sentences. Then write a three- or four-sentence summary of what you think each person is saying.

2. Read your peers' summaries of your own paper. Think about how you could make your ideas clearer. Write down your thoughts or insights in your log.

About All the Readings in This Chapter

PREPARING FOR WRITING

Work with a partner. Choose one activity.

Activity A: The pieces in this chapter describe birth and death, two powerful events in human life. They show how a variety of persons react to these events and the lasting effects birth and death have.

Look back through the pieces and find words, sentences, and paragraphs whereby the people in the stories express their reactions to birth or death and how the event affects them. Make a list on a separate piece of paper, and see what connections you find.

Activity B: We often speak about the birth or death of an idea, an invention, a concept. For example, we talk about the birth of the space age or the end of the time when Western gentlemen opened doors for ladies or offered them their seats on a crowded bus. From your knowledge, make a list of events, ideas, concepts, or inventions that have been born or have died. (Look back at what you wrote about "Death in the Open," p. 106, for ideas.)

Births and deaths of ideas and things may produce similar kinds of feelings and reactions as human birth and death. Next to each thing on your list, write down reactions and feelings people have had to these events.

TOPICS FOR WRITING

Choose one activity.

Activity A: The selection from Ecclesiastes tells us simply that there is a time for birth and death in our lives, that they are natural events. Yet the birth and death of people in our lives affect us strongly, often more than other events. Write about why you think this is so. Use examples and lessons from the stories.

Activity B: The birth and death of ideas, concepts, or inventions may produce similar kinds of strong feelings as the birth and death of human beings. For example, many people welcome the birth of space travel and think it a miracle, just as Jorge Icaza thought the birth of his daughter was a miracle. Or they may not agree with other people who feel that a concept, for example, that a woman's place is in the home, has died. They may disagree, get angry, and keep it alive.

Write about one such birth or death, describing reactions and feelings to it. You can write about a personal experience, or you can describe something you've read about.

Activity C: Look back at the list of words and sentences expressing feelings and reactions to birth and death that you drew up in Activity A of Preparing for Writing. Choose any that interest you. Think about what they mean to you. Do you see a focus or a point that you feel strongly about or have had experience with? Write a composition about it, using material from the readings and from your experience.

AFTER WRITING

1. When you finish, go over your paper with your pen in hand, reading each word aloud so that you can hear it and touching each word with your pen. This proofreading technique will help you to find errors and things that don't sound right. Don't stop until you find at least three things to change. Fix them.

2. Give your piece of writing to two different people to read. Each person should write a response to your composition, telling you:
   a. What they think your main point is
   b. What they like about your piece (form or content)
   c. What they'd like you to add or tell more about

3. Read your readers' responses.

4. Write in your log about how you wrote this piece. Think especially about how you chose your ideas and developed them. Also, did you do anything differently from the way you've written before?

Extra Readings

A Prayer
Buddha

Buddha, an Indian philosopher and the founder of Buddhism, lived about 500 B.C.

Now may every living thing, young or old, weak or strong, living near or far, known or unknown, living or departed or yet unborn, may every living thing be full of bliss.

African Proverb

A proverb is a short saying that expresses a well-known fact or truth.

One is born, one dies; the land increases.

What the Doctor Said
Raymond Carver

Raymond Carver, a writer of fiction and poetry, died in 1988 at the age of 49. This poem was published posthumously.

He said it doesn't look good
he said it looks bad in fact real bad
he said I counted thirty-two of them on one lung before
I quit counting them
I said I'm glad I wouldn't want to know
about any more being there than that
he said are you a religious man do you kneel down
in forest groves and let yourself ask for help
when you come to a waterfall
mist blowing against your face and arms
do you stop and ask for understanding at those moments
I said not yet but I intend to start today
he said I'm real sorry he said
I wish I had some other kind of news to give you
I said Amen and he said something else
I didn't catch and not knowing what else to do
and not wanting him to have to repeat it
and me to have to fully digest it
I just looked at him
for a minute and he looked back it was then
I jumped up and shook hands with this man who'd just given me
something no one else on earth had ever given me
I may even have thanked him habit being so strong

How the Milky Way Came to Be

"How the Milky Way Came to Be" is a South African folktale explaining the creation of the group of stars known as the Milky Way. Folktales are traditional stories of unknown authorship told to the people of a culture to illustrate their traditions, beliefs, and practices or to explain the world around them.

Up there, in the sky, there are billions of stars. No one knows how many, because no one can count them. And to think that among them is a bright road which is made of wood ashes,—nothing else!

Long ago, the sky was pitch black at night, but people learned in time to make fires to light up the darkness.

One night, a young girl, who sat warming herself by a wood fire, played with the ashes. She took the ashes in her hands and threw them up to see how pretty they were when they floated in the air. And as they floated away, she put more wood on the fire and stirred it with a stick. Bright sparks flew everywhere and wafted high, high into the night. They hung in the air and made a bright road across the sky, looking like silver and diamonds.

And there the road is to this day. Some people call it the Milky Way; some call it the Stars' Road, but no matter what you call it, it is the path made by a young girl many, many years ago, who threw the bright sparks of her fire high up into the sky to make a road in the darkness.

No Rainbows, No Roses
Beverly P. Dipo

Beverly Dipo was a student at Utah State University when she wrote this essay, which was chosen as one of the Bedford Prize winners for student writing in 1985. She is a nurse and a writer.

I have never seen Mrs. Trane before, but I know by the report I received from the previous shift that tonight she will die. Making my rounds, I go from room to room, checking other patients first and saving Mrs. Trane for last, not to avoid her, but because she will require the most time to care for.

Everyone else seems to be all right for the time being; they have had their medications, backrubs and are easily settled for the night.

At the door to 309, I pause, adjusting my eyes to the darkness. The only light in the room is coming from an infusion pump, which is flashing its red beacon as if in warning, and the dim hall light that barely confirms the room's furnishings and the shapeless form on the bed. As I stand there, the smell hits my nostrils, and I close my eyes as I remember the stench of rot and decay from past experience. In my mouth I taste the bitter bile churning in the pit of my stomach. I swallow uneasily and cross the room in the dark, reaching for the light switch above the sink, and as it silently illuminates the scene, I return to the bed to observe the patient with a detached, medical routineness.

Mrs. Trane lies motionless: the head seems unusually large on a skeleton frame, and except for a few fine wisps of grey hair around the ears, is bald from the chemotherapy that had offered brief hope; the skin is dark yellow and sags loosely around exaggerated long bones that not even a gown and bedding can disguise; the right arm lies straight out at the side, taped cruelly to a board to secure the IV fluid its access; the left arm is across the sunken chest, which rises and falls in the uneven waves of Cheyne-Stokes respirations; a catheter hanging on the side of the bed is draining thick brown urine from the bladder, the source of the deathly smell.

I reach for the long, thin fingers that are lying on the chest. They are ice cold, and I quickly move to the wrist and feel for the weak, thready pulse. Mrs. Trane's eyes flutter open as her head turns toward me slightly. As she tries to form a word on her dry, parched lips, I bend close to her and scarcely hear as she whispers, "water." Taking a glass of water from the bedside table, I put my finger over the end of the straw and allow a few droplets of the cool moisture to slide into her mouth. She makes no attempt to swallow; there is just not enough strength. "More," the raspy voice says, and we repeat the procedure. This time she does manage to swallow and weakly says, "thank you." I touch her gently in response. She is too weak for conversation, so without asking, I go about providing for her needs, explaining to her in hushed tones each move I make. Picking her up in my arms like a child, I turn her on her side. She is so very small and light. Carefully, I rub lotion into the yellow skin, which rolls freely over the bones, feeling perfectly the outline of each vertebra in the back and the round smoothness of the ileac crest. Placing a pillow between her legs, I notice that these too are ice cold, and not until I run my hand up over her knees do I feel any of the life-giving warmth of blood coursing through fragile veins. I find myself in awe of the life force which continues despite such a state of decomposition.

When I am finished, I pull a chair up beside the bed to face her and taking her free hand between mine, again notice the long, thin fingers. Graceful. There is no jewelry; it would have fallen off long ago. I wonder briefly if she has any family, and then I see that there are neither bouquets of flowers, nor pretty plants on the shelves, no brightly crayon-colored posters of rainbows, nor boastful self-portraits from grandchildren on the walls. There is no hint in the room anywhere, that this is a person who is loved. As though she has been reading my mind, Mrs. Trane answers my thoughts and quietly tells me, "I sent . . . my family . . . home . . . tonight . . . didn't want . . . them . . . to see . . . ." She cannot go on, but knowingly, I have understood what it is she has done. I lower my eyes, not knowing what to say, so I say nothing. Again she seems to sense my unease, "you . . . stay. . . ." Time seems to have come to a standstill. In the total silence, I noticeably feel my own heartbeat quicken and hear my breathing as it begins to match hers, stride for uneven stride. Our eyes meet and somehow, together, we become aware that this is a special moment between us, a moment when two human beings are so close we feel as if our souls touch. Her long fingers curl easily around my hand and I nod my head slowly, smiling. Wordlessly, through yellowed eyes, I receive my thank you and her eyes slowly close.

Some unknown amount of time passes before her eyes open again, only this time there is no response in them, just a blank stare. Without warning, her breathing stops, and within a few moments, the faint pulse is also gone. One single tear flows from her left eye, across the cheekbone and down onto the pillow. I begin to cry quietly. There is a tug of emotion within me for this stranger who so quickly came into and went from my life. Her suffering is done, yet so is the life. Slowly, still holding her hand, I become aware that I do not mind this emotional tug of war, that in fact, it was a privilege she has allowed me, and I would do it again, gladly. Mrs. Trane spared her family an episode that perhaps they were not equipped to handle and instead, shared it with me, knowing somehow that I would handle it and indeed, needed it to grow, both privately and professionally. She had not wanted to have her family see her die, yet she did not want to die alone. No one should die alone, and I am glad I was there for her.

Two days later, I read Mrs. Trane's obituary in the paper. She had been a widow for five years, was the mother of seven, grandmother of eighteen, an active member of her church, a leader of volunteer organizations in her community, college-educated in music, a concert pianist and a piano teacher for over thirty years.

Yes, they were long and graceful fingers.

Chapter 4

Personal Growth and Change

1. In your log, freewrite for 5 minutes about the meaning of the title of this chapter.

2. Look at the cartoon. Then freewrite for a few more minutes.

3. Reread what you wrote. Write one sentence that states an important idea you wrote about.

4. Read your sentence to your group.

BEFORE READING

1. The title of this chapter is "Personal Growth and Change." What kind of a journey would you expect to read about in a poem in this chapter? Write a sentence in your reading log.

2. Read "The Journey."

The Journey
Mary Oliver

This poem is from a collection called Dream Work.

One day you finally knew
what you had to do, and began,
though the voices around you
kept shouting
their bad advice—
though the whole house
began to tremble
and you felt the old tug
at your ankles.
"Mend my life!"
each voice cried.
But you didn't stop.
You knew what you had to do,
though the wind pried
with its stiff fingers
at the very foundations—
though their melancholy
was terrible.
It was already late
enough, and a wild night,
and the road full of fallen
branches and stones.
But little by little,
as you left their voices behind,
the stars began to burn
through the sheets of clouds,
and there was a new voice,

which you slowly
recognized as your own,
that kept you company
as you strode deeper and deeper
into the world,
determined to do
the only thing you could do—
determined to save
the only life you could save.

AFTER READING

1. Write a sentence in your reading log that summarizes the meaning of the poem as you understand it. Compare it with what another person wrote.

2. The person in the poem has to struggle not only with people but also with elements of nature. Underline all of the natural forces and objects that get in the person's way. In your log, write a response to the words you underlined. How do they make you feel?

3. Imagine that you are making a movie of this poem. How many actors would you have to hire? How many scenes would you need? What kinds of props and special effects would you have to have? List them with a partner. Report to the whole class. Your teacher or one student can write a combined list of actors, scenes, props, and special effects on the board.

HOW IT'S WRITTEN

1. Choose one activity. Make sure that at least one person in your group takes each one.

   Activity A: English teachers often tell their students not to use *you* in their compositions because a writer can't always be sure that the reader has had the experience or feelings being talked about or because it sounds too much like the language of advertising, as in "You can have it all." In this poem, Mary Oliver breaks that rule. Why does she do this? What effect does she achieve by using *you*? How does it make you feel?

Activity B: Oliver could have written this poem in a paragraph, like this:

One day you finally knew what you had to do, and began, though the voices around you kept shouting their bad advice—though the whole house began to tremble and you felt the old tug at your ankles. "Mend my life!" each voice cried. But you didn't stop. You knew what you had to do, though the wind pried with its stiff fingers at the very foundations—though their melancholy was terrible. It was already late enough, and a wild night, and the road full of fallen branches and stones. But little by little, as you left their voices behind, the stars began to burn through the sheets of clouds, and there was a new voice, which you slowly recognized as your own, that kept you company as you strode deeper and deeper into the world, determined to do the only thing you could do—determined to save the only life you could save.

Why didn't she?

Activity C: In this poem, Oliver uses concrete, specific language to describe a figurative rather than a literal journey. That is, the journey takes place in the mind of the person she describes, and yet Oliver describes it as if it were taking place outdoors. Why?

2. Discuss what you learned with your group.

TOPICS FOR WRITING

Choose one activity.

Activity A: Write, as a poem or a composition, the next stage of the journey. What do "you" do next? Continue using the same kind of symbolic language Oliver does.

Activity B: This poem begins at the moment in life when a person realizes that the old voices must be left behind and one's own voice must be heeded instead. Have you had an experience of leaving old voices behind and listening to yourself? Was there a time when you stopped listening to the advice of your parents, religion, teachers, or culture and began to make your own decisions, even at the risk of disappointing others? Write a composition about how a person makes such a decision, using your experience as an example.

AFTER WRITING

Read what you wrote to your group. Ask group members to tell you one strength in your writing and one thing that was not clear to them.

BEFORE READING
---

1. Read the introductory information and the saying at the beginning of the essay. What connections do you see between the saying and what you know so far about "Stories"? Talk about this with your group.
2. Read the essay.

Stories
Gloria Anzaldúa from her book
Borderlands/La Frontera

An essay by Gloria Anzaldúa describes how her Mexican heritage affects her writing. In this, the first part of the essay, Anzaldúa tells of her beginnings as a storyteller and writer.

"Out of poverty, poetry;
out of suffering, song."
—A MEXICAN SAYING

When I was seven, eight, nine, fifteen, sixteen years old, I would read in bed with a flashlight under the covers, hiding my self-imposed insomnia from my mother. I preferred the world of the imagination to the death of sleep. My sister, Hilda, who slept in the same bed with me, would threaten to tell my mother unless I told her a story.

I was familiar with *cuentos*—my grandmother told stories like the one about her getting on top of the roof while down below rabid coyotes were ravaging the place and wanting to get at her. My father told stories about a phantom giant dog that appeared out of nowhere and sped along the side of the pickup no matter how fast he was driving.

Nudge a Mexican and she or he will break out with a story. So, huddling under the covers, I made up stories for my sister night after night. After a while she wanted two stories per night. I learned to give her installments, building up the suspense with convoluted complications until the story climaxed several nights later. It must have been then that I decided to put stories on paper. It must have been then that working with images and writing became connected to night.

AFTER READING

1. In your log, freewrite for a few minutes about what you just read. Share your writing with your group.

2. As a group, write down one question you have about the passage. Discuss your question with the class.

HOW IT'S WRITTEN

1. Find one sentence in the essay that you like or that you find especially well written. Copy the sentence on the left side of a page in your log. On the right side of the same page, write about why you like the sentence or what makes the sentence well written.

2. Read what you wrote to your group. Discuss your findings with the class.

TOPICS FOR WRITING

Choose one activity.

Activity A: Telling stories when she was a child helped Anzaldúa decide to be a writer. How did you choose your present or future career? Tell the story of how this happened.

Activity B: Storytelling was an important part of Anzaldúa's growing up. Was storytelling important in your personal growth? Was there another activity that was more important, for example, song, poetry, dance? Write a composition explaining the role of one such activity in your life.

Activity C: Anzaldúa chose a Mexican saying to begin her essay. Think of a saying in your native language that captures an important value in your culture. Translate the saying, and write a composition explaining and illustrating its significance.

AFTER WRITING

1. Give your paper to another person for feedback. Ask the person to tell the important point and to select one or two sentences that the

person likes or that are especially well written and tell why he or she chose them.

2. Read your writing to your group.

3. Write in your log about *how* you wrote this piece. For example, what was easy? What was hard? How many times did you write it? What did you change, if anything? Why?

BEFORE READING

1. Make a **cluster** around the words "seventeen-year-olds." Write those words in the center of a page of your log. Then, all around that phrase, in any arrangement that makes sense to you, write down words and phrases that describe the feelings of seventeen-year-olds. (See Appendix A.2, p. 204, for explanation and examples of clustering.)

   Share your notebook page with a partner. If your partner does not understand why you put down a particular word or phrase, explain the connection.

2. Read the title, introductory information, and date of this journal piece.

3. Circle one or two words in your cluster you think might appear in Plath's journal entry. Then read the passage.

Reflections of a Seventeen-Year-Old
Sylvia Plath

Sylvia Plath was born in Boston in 1932 and died by suicide in England in 1963. She wrote several books of poetry, a children's book, and the well-known novel The Bell Jar. *Plath kept a journal in which she recorded thoughts about herself, comments to herself, details of places she visited, and discussions of difficulties in her writing. The following selection, written when Plath was 17, is one of her earliest diary entries.*

November 13, 1949

As of today I have decided to keep a diary again—just a place where I can write my thoughts and opinions when I have a moment. Somehow I have to keep and hold the rapture of being seventeen. Every day is so precious I feel infinitely sad at the thought of all this time melting farther and farther away from me as I grow older. *Now, now* is the perfect time of my life.

In reflecting back upon these last sixteen years, I can see tragedies and happiness, all relative—all unimportant now—fit only to smile upon a bit mistily.

I still do not know myself. Perhaps I never will. But I feel free—unbound by responsibility, I still can come up to my own private room, with my drawings hanging on the walls . . . and pictures pinned up over my bureau. It is a room suited to me—tailored, uncluttered and peaceful. . . . I love the quiet lines of the furniture, the two bookcases filled with poetry books and fairy tales saved from childhood.

At the present moment I am very happy, sitting at my desk, looking out at the bare trees around the house across the street. . . . Always I want to be an observer. I want to be affected by life deeply, but never so blinded that I cannot see my share of existence in a wry, humorous light and mock myself as I mock others.

I am afraid of getting older. I am afraid of getting married. Spare me from cooking three meals a day—spare me from the relentless cage of routine and rote. I want to be free—free to know people and their backgrounds—free to move to different parts of the world, so I may learn that there are other morals and standards besides my own. I want, I think, to be omniscient. . . . I think I would like to call myself "The girl who wanted to be God." Yet if I were not in this body, where *would* I be? Perhaps I am *destined* to be classified and qualified. But oh, I cry out against it. I am I—I am powerful—but to what extent? I am I.

Sometimes I try to put myself in another's place, and I am frightened when I find I am almost succeeding. How awful to be anyone but I. I have a terrible egotism. I love my flesh, my face, my limbs, with overwhelming devotion. I know that I am "too tall" and have a fat nose, and yet I pose and prink before the mirror, seeing more and more how lively I am. . . . I have erected in my mind an image of myself—idealistic and beautiful. Is not that image, free from blemish, the true self—the true perfection? Am I wrong when this image insinuates itself between me and the merciless mirror? (Oh, even now I glance back on what I have just written—how foolish it sounds, how overdramatic.)

Never, never, never will I reach the perfection I long for with all my soul—my paintings, my poems, my stories—all poor, poor reflections . . . for I have been too thoroughly conditioned to the conventional surroundings of this community . . . my vanity desires luxuries which I can never have. . . .

I am continually more aware of the power which change plays in my life. . . .There will come a time when I must face myself at last. Even now I dread the big choices which loom up in my life—what college? what career? I am afraid. I feel uncertain. What is best for me? What do I want? I do not know. I love freedom. I deplore constrictions and limitations. . . . I am not as wise as I have thought. I can see, as from a valley, the roads lying open for me, but I cannot see the end—the consequences. . . .

Oh, I love *now*, with all my fears and forebodings, for now I still am not completely molded. My life is still just beginning. I am strong. I long for a cause to devote my energies to.

AFTER READING

1. In your log, freewrite for 5 minutes about what you just read. Share your writing with a partner.

2. a. Reread the piece, and *circle* all the words that the writer used to describe her feelings. Were any of these words ones you wrote in the cluster you did for Before Reading 1? Talk about your observations with your group.

   b. As a group, divide the words you circled into two categories: positive and negative. Make two lists in your notebook. Can you find words that are opposites? Connect them with arrows.

   c. Write for 3 minutes in your log about what you found. Read your writing to the class.

HOW I READ IT

How did looking at words expressing feelings help you understand this piece better? Talk about this with the class.

HOW IT'S WRITTEN

1. Reread one or two essays from earlier chapters (for example, "Sometimes Home Is Not Really Home," "A Story of Conflicts," or "Death in the Open"). With your group, compare Plath's journal entry to an essay. How are they different? Similar? Look at topic, writing style, organization, and so on.

2. With the class, list some characteristics of *journals* and some characteristics of *essays*.

TOPICS FOR WRITING

Choose one activity.

Activity A: Write "_____-year-olds" in the center of a page of your log. Fill in the blank with your age. Then around this phrase, write words or phrases expressing feelings you associate with being this age. Next, write a journal entry that focuses on some of the feelings you have now at this time in your life. The title of your piece will be "Reflections of a _____-Year-Old." Make it look like a journal entry.

Activity B: Find one sentence from Plath's diary to use as the first sentence of a composition about yourself.

Activity C: Plath's journal entry expresses the different and sometimes conflicting feelings of many teenagers: sadness and happiness, fear and power. Write a letter of reassurance or encouragement to a teenager you know who is experiencing similar turmoil.

AFTER WRITING

1. Read your writing aloud to your group. Ask for feedback: What did they understand? What do they like best about the writing?

2. As a group, choose one piece to read to the class.

BEFORE READING

1. Make a list of some skills you've learned outside school, either at home, at work, or at play.

2. Read the introductory information about the poem. Then read the poem as many times as you wish.

Growing Up Outdoors: Young Hunter
A. and B. Hungry Wolf

This poem tells how a Native American boy learns to hunt. It is an example of the traditional way of teaching in Native American communities.

They went outside.
In the clean snow,
    Grandfather made
    some turkey tracks.
Young Hunter was excited.
    "I've seen those.
I know what they are," he shouted
    and off he started running,
    holding out in front of him
    his bow and arrow.

Grandfather called after him,
    "Are you picking berries
    with the women
    that you need to make such noise?
Perhaps you shout
    to warn the game away
    from such a dangerous hunter."

Young Hunter came back.
He stopped running and shouting.
He watched his grandfather.

He watched him taking quiet steps.
Then he, too, took quiet steps
and together they went
hunting for turkey.

AFTER READING

1. Write down one or two things you understand from the poem and one or two things you don't understand. Share and discuss your writing with two other people.

2. With your two partners, read the poem aloud: One person reads Young Hunter's words, the second person reads Grandfather's words, and the third reads the rest of the poem.

3. With your two partners, make separate lists of the actions in the poem (words and phrases) that go with Grandfather, Young Hunter, and both. Make an observation about the words in each list.

4. In your reading log, list the lessons you get out of this poem. Share your list with your two partners, then with the class.

TOPICS FOR WRITING

Choose one activity.

Activity A: Recall a particular time when you learned how to do something outside school that made you proud. (Look back at your list in Before Reading for ideas.) Tell what you learned and how, including details about who, what, where, when, and why it made you proud.

Activity B: Tell how you or someone you know learned a skill as Young Hunter did. Tell it as a short story, a parable, or a poem similar to this one. Use quotations if you can. You don't have to write many words; instead, describe the characters and the event in a few carefully chosen words.

Activity C: Young Hunter was willing to follow his grandfather's advice. Do young people today follow the advice of their elders? Support your opinion with examples from your experience and reading.

AFTER WRITING

1. Before you read your piece of writing to your group, decide what kind of feedback you'd like to get. For example, "Tell me if you like it." "Is everything clear?" "Do you like the ending?" Dictate your questions to your group.

2. Read your piece of writing aloud. Then ask everyone to write a response to your request for feedback. If there's time, the others can share their responses aloud before giving them to you. See if they are similar or different.

3. In your log, write one or two things you learned about your writing today.

BEFORE READING
---

1. Read the introductory information about this piece. Write down some words you associate with a slum. Share them with the class. What do you think the title means? Talk about this with the class.

2. Locate Brazil and São Paulo on a map.

3. Read the translator's preface to *Child of the Dark.*

Child of the Dark: Carolina Maria de Jesus
David St. Clair

> Child of the Dark *is a translation of the diaries of Carolina Maria de Jesus, a Brazilian woman who lived in a* favela, *or slum, of São Paulo.*

TRANSLATOR'S PREFACE

Carolina Maria de Jesus came to the favela of Canindé in 1947. She was unemployed and pregnant. No one wanted her. Her lover had abandoned her and the white family where she worked as a maid refused to let her in the house. She was desperate and turned to the favela. Carrying boards on her head from the construction site of a church five miles away, she built a shack, roofed it with flattened tin cans and cardboard. Three months later her son João was born. Then began the fight for survival that only ceased with the publication of her diary.

Carolina was born in 1913 in the little town of Sacramento in the state of Minas Gerais, in the interior of Brazil. Her mother, an unmarried farm hand, was worried about her daughter having the same kind of life and insisted that Carolina attend school. The little girl hated it, and every morning her mother practically had to spank her all the way to the one-room building. It was only when she learned to read, three months after opening day, that she enjoyed her education.

"It was a Wednesday, and when I left school I saw a paper with some writing on it. It was an announcement of the local movie house. 'Today. Pure Blood. Tom Mix.'

"I shouted happily—'I can read! I can read!' "

She wandered through the streets reading aloud the labels in the drugstore window and the names of the stores.

For the next two years Carolina was first in her class. Then her mother got a better job on a farm far away from Sacramento and Carolina had to give up her beloved school. She never went back. Her education stopped at the second grade. . . .

Carolina built her shack [in the favela] like the others there. When it rained the water came in the roof, rotting her one mattress and rusting the few pots and pans. There was a sack over the window that she'd pull for privacy and late at night she would light a small kerosene lamp "and cover my nose with a rag to take away some of the favela stench.". . .

In order to keep from thinking about her troubles she started to write. . . . Her notebooks were those she found in the trash, writing on the clean side of the page with a treasured fountain pen, making slow even letters.

Her neighbors knew of her writings and made fun of them. Most of them couldn't even read, but thought she should be doing other things with her spare time than writing and saving old notebooks. They called her "Dona" (Madame) Carolina. . . . Carolina's life was miserable but she refused to lower the standards she had set for herself and her children and mingle with those she couldn't stand. . . .

In April of 1958, Audalio Dantas, a young reporter, was covering the inauguration of a playground near Canindé for his newspaper. When the politicians had made their speeches and gone away, the grown men of the favela began fighting with the children for a place on the teeter-totters and swings. Carolina, standing in the crowd, shouted furiously: "If you continue mistreating these children, I'm going to put all your names in my book!"

Interested, the reporter asked the tall black woman about her book. At first she didn't want to talk to him, but slowly he won her confidence and she took him to her shack. There in the bottom drawer of a dilapidated dresser she pulled out her cherished notebooks. . . .

Dantas persuaded her to let him take one of the notebooks—there were twenty-six of them covering a three-year span—to his newspaper. And the next day while the story on the playground got small notice, a two-column full-length excerpt from Carolina's diary appeared.

The story electrified the town. . . .

Shortly after this Dantas was offered the important position of chief of the São Paulo bureau of O Cruzeiro magazine, Brazil's biggest weekly. Here, he saw an even better opportunity to bring the story of Carolina's life to the attention of all Brazilians. For one full year he worked on her notebooks, . . . concentrating on her diary, extracting the best of each day. Published, her diary became the literary sensation of Brazil.

Never had a book such an impact on Brazil. In three days the first printing of 10,000 copies was sold out in São Paulo alone. In less than six months 90,000 copies were sold in Brazil and today it is still on the best-seller list, having sold more than any other Brazilian book in history. . . .

AFTER READING

1. Choose one activity.

   Activity A: Write a double entry in your log.

   Activity B: Write answers to these questions:

   What do you understand or see in what you read?

   How do you feel about what you understand?

   What do you associate with your understanding?

2. Pass your notebook to a partner for a written response. (Write directly in your partner's notebook.)
   Read your partner's response.

3. With a partner, draw a *time line* of Carolina's life. (That is, draw a line along which you put the major events of Carolina's life with approximate dates or ages.) Circle the *turning points* in her life (the events that dramatically changed her life).
   Share your time line with your group. Discuss your time lines with the class. Then read the diaries.

Child of the Dark: The Diary of Carolina Maria de Jesus

1955

July 19 . . . I am living in a favela. But if God helps me, I'll get out of here. I hope the politicians tear down the favelas. There are people who take advantage of the way they live to bully those weaker than themselves. There is a house here that has five children and an old woman who walks the entire day begging. There are wives that when their husbands are ill go out and support the family. The husbands, when they see their wives taking care of the home, never get well again. . . .

Today was a blessed day for me. The troublemakers of the favela see that I'm writing and know that it's about them. They decided to leave me in peace. In the favelas the men are more tolerant, more understanding. The rowdies are the women. Their intrigues . . . grate against the nerves. My nerves can't stand it. But I'm strong. I don't let anything bother me deeply. I don't get discouraged. . . .

1958

May 2 I'm not lazy. There are times when I try to keep up my diary. But then I think it's not worth it and figure I'm wasting my time.

I've made a promise to myself. I want to treat people that I know with more consideration. I want to have a pleasant smile for children and the employed.

I received a summons to appear at 8 p.m. at police station number 12. I spent the day looking for paper. At night my feet pained me so I couldn't walk. It started to rain. I went to the station and took José Carlos with me. The summons was for him. José Carlos is nine years old.

May 3 I went to the market at Carlos de Campos Street looking for any old thing. I got a lot of greens. But it didn't help much, for I've got no cooking fat. The children are upset because there's nothing to eat.

May 6 In the morning I went for water. I made João carry it. I was happy, then I received another summons. I was inspired yesterday and my verses were so pretty, I forgot to go to the station. It was 11:00 when I remembered the invitation from the illustrious lieutenant of the 12th precinct.

My advice to would-be politicians is that people do not tolerate hunger. It's necessary to know hunger to know how to describe it. . . .

May 10 I went to the police station and talked to the lieutenant. What a pleasant man! If I had known he was going to be so pleasant, I'd have gone on the first summons. The lieutenant was interested in my boys' education. He said the favelas have an unhealthy atmosphere where the people have more chance to go wrong than to become useful to state and country. I thought: if he knows this why doesn't he make a report and send it to the politicians? . . . Now he tells me this, I a poor garbage collector. I can't even solve my own problems.

Brazil needs to be led by a person who has known hunger. Hunger is also a teacher.

Who has gone hungry learns to think of the future and of the children. . . .

May 20 Day was breaking when I got out of bed. Vera woke up and sang and asked me to sing with her. We sang. Then José Carlos and João joined in.

The morning was damp and foggy. The sun was rising but its heat didn't chase away the cold. I stayed thinking: there are seasons when the sun dominates. There's a season for the rain. There's a season for the wind. Now is the time for the cold. Among them there are no rivalries. Each one has a time.

I opened the window and watched the women passing by with their coats discolored and worn by time. It won't be long until these coats which they got from others, and which should be in a museum, will be replaced by others. The politicians must give us things. That includes me too, because I'm also a *favelado*. I'm one of the discarded. I'm in the garbage dump and those in the garbage dump either burn themselves or throw themselves into ruin. . . .

Sometimes families move into the favela with children. In the beginning they are educated, friendly. Days later they use foul language, are mean and quarrelsome. They are diamonds turned to lead. They are transformed from objects that were in the living room to objects banished to the garbage dump.

For me the world instead of evolving is turning primitive. Those who don't know hunger will say: "Whoever wrote this is crazy." But who has gone hungry can say:

"Well, Dona Carolina. The basic necessities must be within reach of everyone."

How horrible it is to see a child eat and ask: "Is there more?" This word "more" keeps ringing in the mother's head as she looks in the pot and doesn't have any more.

When a politician tells us in his speeches that he is on the side of the people, that he is only in politics in order to improve our living conditions, asking for our votes, promising to freeze prices, he is well aware that by touching on these grave problems he will win at the polls. Afterward he divorces himself from the people. He looks at them with half-closed eyes, and with a pride that hurts us. . . .

June 2 . . . In the morning I'm always nervous. I'm afraid of not getting money to buy food to eat. But today is Monday and there is a lot of paper in the streets. Senhor Manuel showed up saying he wanted to marry me. But I don't want to, because I'm in my maturity. And later a man isn't going to like a woman who can't stop reading and gets out of bed to write and sleeps with paper and pencil under her pillow. That's why I prefer to live alone, for my ideals. He gave me 50 cruzeiros and I paid the seamstress for a dress that she made for Vera. Dona Alice came by complaining that Senhor Alexandre was insulting her because of 65 cruzeiros. I thought: ah money! It kills and it makes hate take root.

June 3   When I was at the streetcar stop Vera started to cry. She wanted a cookie. I only had ten cruzeiros, two for the streetcar and eight to buy hamburger. Dona Geralda gave me four cruzeiros for me to buy the cookies. She ate and sang. I thought: my problem is always food! I took the streetcar and Vera started to cry because she didn't want to stand up, and there wasn't any place to sit down.

When I have little money I try not to think of children who are going to ask for bread. Bread and coffee. I sent my thoughts toward the sky. I thought: can it be that people live up there? Are they better than us? Can it be that they have an advantage over us? Can it be that nations up there are as different as nations on earth? Or is there just one nation? I wonder if the favela exists there? And if up there a favela does exist, can it be that when I die I'm going to live in a favela? . . .

June 12   I left the bed at 3 a.m. because when one is not sleepy he starts to think of the misery around him. I got out of bed to write. When I write I think I live in a golden castle that shines in the sunlight. The windows are silver and the panes are diamonds. My view is overlooking a garden and I gaze on flowers of all kinds. I must create this atmosphere of fantasy to forget that I am in a favela.

I made coffee and went for water. The stars were in the heavens. How disgusting it is to step in mud.

My happy hours are when I am living in my imaginary castles.

AFTER READING

1. Freewrite for 5 minutes about what you read.

2. Reread the diary, looking for one paragraph or one entry that is especially powerful or that especially strikes you. Write for 3 minutes about it. Then read the paragraph or entry aloud to your group and talk about your response to it.

3. With your group, make a list of some of the topics Carolina writes about. What do you learn about Carolina's life through these excerpts from her diaries? About her as a person? Make one list of adjectives you could use to describe her life and another list you could use to describe her character. Share your lists with the class.

HOW IT'S WRITTEN

1. Look at the list of topics you made for After Reading 3. Then look back at Sylvia Plath's journal entry ("Reflections of a Seventeen-

Year-Old," p. 123). Do you see any similarities in topic? In style? Do you see any differences? Talk about this with your group and then with the class.

2. Write a journal entry of your own, dating it with today's date. Share your entry with a partner.

3. What use might journal writing be to you as a writer? Talk about this with the class.

TOPICS FOR WRITING

Choose one activity.

Activity A: The translator, in his preface to *Child of the Dark*, describes Carolina's excitement when she learned to read. He also talks about how Carolina used writing to keep from thinking about her troubles. These two skills, reading and writing, gave Carolina personal power and certainly helped change her life. Write an essay about the power of reading and/or writing. Use yourself, Carolina, or anyone else you know of as examples.

Activity B: Do people make changes, or do changes just happen to them? Or both? How do you characterize Carolina's change? Explain your answer to the first question in writing. If you wish, use Carolina (or anyone else in this book) as an example.

Activity C: The publication of Carolina's diaries was a turning point in her life; she became famous, and she was able to move out of the *favela*. Has there been a turning point in your life or a point at which your life changed dramatically, either because of something you did or because of something that happened to you? Explain what this turning point was, describing yourself both before and after the change.

AFTER WRITING

1. Put your composition away for a day or two. Then reread it as though you were a reader. Write a summary sentence of each paragraph. Then answer these questions:
   a. What important point is the piece making?
   b. Does each paragraph concentrate on one aspect of the topic? Does each paragraph relate to and develop the important point?

    c. Does each paragraph connect with the paragraph before it?

    d. Does the last paragraph "wrap it up" in some way?

2. Share your writing with your group. Then choose one composition to read to the class.

3. Write for a few minutes about how you wrote this piece. For example, did writing summary sentences of each paragraph help you? Did answering the questions help you? How?

BEFORE READING

1. Read the introductory information.

2. Skim the passage. Note the breaks, dividing the piece into four sections; read the first sentence of each section. Based on your skimming, write down one or two questions you expect the piece to answer. Share your questions with the class.

3. As you read these excerpts, when you get to a break and at the end, write a quick response in your log: a question, a thought, an idea, a feeling, an association, an observation about your reading process.

My Way or Theirs?
Liu Zongren

During his two years in the United States as a visiting journalist, Liu Zongren found many customs and attitudes different from those of his native Chinese culture. Some of these strange customs he rejected; others he accepted, at least in part. In his book Two Years in the Melting Pot, *he shows us that he was personally affected and often changed by his experience in a foreign land. Here he writes about table manners, clothes, raising children, and going home.*

TABLE MANNERS

There were many American customs which puzzled me. I was very impatient with table formality. Why do people have to remember to change plates, forks, knives, and spoons so many times in one meal? I was especially bothered by that piece of cloth called a napkin. English gentlemen tuck a white napkin under their chins during a meal and Americans put one on their laps. I had trouble remembering to do this even a year and a half after I had arrived and had been to a number of fancy restaurants. Even if I did place it on my lap, it always slipped onto the floor. I often remembered to use my napkin only when I saw someone wipe his mouth with one; I then hastily picked mine up and spread it across my lap, stealing a look to see if others had noticed my lack of etiquette.

CLOTHES

The concept of [the Mao] jacket conforms with the Chinese teaching of modesty, taught very early to children. They are told not to differ from others in appearance, not to be conspicuous, or they will provoke gossip. "She is frivolous," people might say if a woman did her hair in a fancy way; or, if she wore western clothing, they might comment, "Her blouse is too open at the neck!"

Of course, this is not the way Americans judge each other. Everyone tries to be different—and sometimes this goes to an extreme. One morning I glanced out of a classroom window to see a bright-colored figure walking across the lawn in front of University Hall. The sun glistened on her scarlet dress and bright red boots; her huge gold earrings sparkled, yet the part that caught the sunshine most was her hair. It was dyed half-red and half-yellow. In China, even a crazy woman would not dare walk out in the open looking like that.

In America, the overriding need to be recognized as an individual is so often expressed in the way one dresses. The exceptions are the teenagers who choose to dress alike and happily submit to the styles dictated by their peers. Parents and schools may not approve of certain fads in clothing yet they find it virtually impossible to control the dress codes. Other than the teenagers, I discovered no restrictions on how people should dress. I never saw two persons dressed identically, except by choice; the businessmen and bank workers on LaSalle Street dressed in three-piece suits and ties, all wearing their wing-tipped shoes. Still, they had enough variety in their outfits to appear different from one another. A young professor at Circle wore a different tie and shirt every day, even if he wore the same suit. With all the clothing changes they made every day, there was little chance that two professors would show up looking alike. . . .

I bought few clothes in the United States, not wanting to spend two hundred dollars for a suit I would never wear back in China. Most of my western Chicago clothes would go into a storage trunk, as my father's had—mere reminders of his ten-year period of service abroad. I wore the same jacket and two pairs of pants all through the seasons, just as I had in Beijing. I thought little of this until two Chinese colleagues from Illinois State University told me they felt embarrassed when they wore the same clothes two days in a row. "Everyone in America changes every day," they said. "We don't have many clothes but we don't want to look shabby. We learned a trick—don't laugh at us. We take off the clothes we wear today and hang them in the closet. Tomorrow we put on another set. The day after tomorrow, we will wear the first set again; then next day, we mix the two sets up and we thus have a new set of clothes."

I laughed, not at my two colleagues, but at people who spend time worrying about what clothes they should wear. It is a waste of time for people to fuss over clothes, and it is also a waste for Chinese to try to find ways to restrict others' manner of dress. I hope that Chinese society will become more open, as America is, about the matter of clothing. A few western suits and blue jeans can hardly change centuries of Chinese teaching—history has already proved that. A billion people are like an immense ocean which can easily accomodate a few drops of foreign pigment without changing color. Western life is very appealing to many young Chinese today, who think that a better life can be achieved by adopting western life-styles. Let them try—they will soon learn.

RAISING CHILDREN

[A Chinese woman who sold stamps at the World's Fair in Knoxville] suggested that I watch how [American] parents reacted when children chose stamps. "The adults never interfere," she said. "If they agree to buy stamps, they just let the children choose on their own. They don't even give opinions. They only pay for them." At the bookstand I later observed that children had just as much freedom in selecting books. The parents interfered with their children's choices only when a parent didn't want to pay for the selected volume.

Most Chinese parents help their children select purchases. They love their children as much as any parent does, and they like to buy things for them. After a Chinese mother has agreed to pay for an item, she lets her child make a choice. Then she says, "This one is no good," or "That one is better than this one." If the child insists on the one he or she has chosen and it is not to the liking of the mother, more often than not the mother will refuse to buy the thing at all. Those mothers who give too much independence to their children are not considered good mothers by Chinese standards. "She spoils her son too much," her neighbor or colleagues will say.

I like the way American parents treat their children. The young ones are treated as small adults—that's why, I think, Americans are so much more independent than Chinese. In Chicago, I had noticed that parents often left their young children with baby-sitters while they went to a party or to the theater. Chinese parents seldom do that. I made a mental note that, after I got back to China, I would give my son more freedom in deciding his own affairs. My wife is too dominating in this respect. I would persuade her to follow American parental practices.

GOING HOME

Home now meant much more than just my wife and our son. It also meant the life I was born into, the surroundings and environment that looked Chinese, the people with whom I shared a culture, and the job at my office which I had, in the past, sometimes resented. I longed for them all. As one Chinese saying goes, all water returns to the sea; all leaves go back to their roots. My roots were in China, in Beijing, in my family. It was time I went home. . . .

I reflected on the fact that most of the successful Chinese I had met in Chicago—doctors and professors—never thought of themselves as Americans. "China is my country. Someday I will go back," one professor told me. These Chinese have a deeper sense of homeland than members of other ethnic groups I met in the United States. They have preserved more ancient Chinese customs and traditions than have the Chinese on either the mainland or Taiwan. It appears easier for a European immigrant to adjust to American society; a Chinese always thinks of his homeland. It is not merely a difference of skin color; it is cultural. I was glad to have become more aware of the importance of upholding my cultural values. . . .

After twenty months of observing American life, I had become more satisfied with the idea of my simple life in China, and I hoped that our country would never be one in which money is of first importance. I would never in my lifetime have the many possessions my middle-class American friends have. Yet, it seemed to me as if they were really only living the same cycle of life that I do in China, except on a higher economic rung of the ladder. We shared the same fundamental needs: family, friends, a familiar culture.

AFTER READING

1. Share the responses you wrote in your log with your group.

2. With a partner, choose one activity.

   Activity A: Write a one-sentence summary of each of the four sections. Share your findings with the class.

   Activity B: Look at the first three sections. For each, tell how Liu was affected by his encounters with American attitudes and customs. Share your findings with the class.

3. Choose a sentence or paragraph that interests you. In your notebook, write a brief response to it, explaining why this part strikes you. Pass your notebook to your partner for a written response.

HOW IT'S WRITTEN

1. Working with your group, look at the first section, "Table Manners." What's the **purpose** of the first sentence? (What does it *do*?) The second sentence? The third? (See Appendix B.4, p. 217, for more information on what sentences can do.) How are these three sentences related to each other? To the rest of the paragraph? Find another paragraph in which Liu uses an example. Talk about how he leads into the example and what the purpose of the example is.

2. Discuss your findings with the class.

3. Write down one thing you learned about writing from these activities.

TOPICS FOR WRITING

Choose one activity.

Activity A: Near the end of this passage, Liu says: "I was glad to have become more aware of the importance of upholding my cultural values." Are there cultural values you have decided are important to uphold (keep) after experiencing a new and strange culture? List some of them. Choose several and write about them, telling what they are and why you think the way you do.

Activity B: At the beginning of this excerpt, Liu says, "There were many American customs which puzzled me." Use that idea as the basis of a composition about yourself and another culture.

Activity C: Liu made a conscious decision to accept some American customs and practices, such as treatment of children. What customs and practices have you adopted—or been forced to adopt—as a result of living in a new culture? Write about these, telling what they are and how they've changed you.

AFTER WRITING

1. Exchange papers with another person. Analyze your partner's use of examples:
   a. What important point is the writer making?
   b. What examples does the writer include?
   c. Do the examples illustrate the writer's important point? (Are they appropriate?)
   d. Is there a place where another example could be added?
2. Read your partner's comments. Then share your writing with your group.

BEFORE READING

1. What words come to your mind when you see the word *stress*? Write down those words. As a class, put all the words on the chalkboard.

2. How would you fill in the blank in this sentence?

   I had a _____ stressful year last year.

   Share what you wrote with your partner. Talk about why you wrote the answer you did.

3. Read the passage about the stress test. Then read the stress scale and figure out your stress score.

A Scale of Stresses
Susan Ovellette Kobasa

The scale of stresses can tell you approximately how much stress you have had in the past year. However, it won't tell you how you handled it. The scale, which was developed by medical researchers Thomas Holmes and Richard Rahe, is used in studies on stress.

In the 1960s, medical researchers Thomas Holmes and Richard Rahe developed a popular scale, which you may have seen, that was a checklist of stressful events. They appreciated the tricky point that *any* major change can be stressful. Negative events like "serious illness of a family member" and "trouble with boss" were high on the list, but so were some positive life-changing events, like marriage. You might want to take the Holmes-Rahe test to find out how much pressure you're under. But remember that the score does not reflect how you deal with stress—it only shows how much you have to deal with. And we now know that the way you handle these events dramatically affects your chances of staying healthy.

By the early 1970s, hundreds of similar studies had followed Holmes and Rahe. And millions of Americans who work and live under stress worried over the reports. Somehow, the research got boiled down to a memorable message. Women's magazines ran headlines like "Stress causes illness!" If you want to stay physically and mentally healthy, the articles said, avoid stressful events.

But such simplistic advice is impossible to follow. Even if stressful events are dangerous, many—like the death of a loved one—are impossible to avoid. Moreover, any warning to avoid *all* stressful events is a prescription for staying away from opportunities as well as trouble. Since any change can be stressful, a person who wanted to be completely free of stress would never marry, have a child, take a new job or move.

The notion that all stress makes you sick also ignores a lot of what we know about people. It assumes we're all vulnerable and passive in the face of adversity. But what about human resilience, initiative and creativity? Many come through periods of stress with more physical and mental vigor than they had before. We also know that a long time without change or challenge can lead to boredom, and physical and mental strain.

[Now turn to the chart on pp. 146–47.]

AFTER READING

1. Write in your journal for a few minutes about what you just read and did. What stresses did you have, and how did you score? How do you feel about it? Were you surprised?

2. Read through the passage accompanying the text again. Underline some sentences that you think are important to remember after finding out your score. Share the sentences you underlined with your partner.

3. If you wish, share your score with your group, and report to your group the stresses you had. Compile a group list of stresses, noting the number of people in the group who had the same stress. Which stresses were most common?

   Report your group's list to the class.

4. Choose one activity.

   Activity A: Are there any stresses that you or your group did not name or don't understand? Find out if anyone in the class can explain them. If not, try to find out before the next class. Then report to the whole class.

   Activity B: With your partner, pick a character from one of the earlier readings in this book, and see how he or she would rate on the scale. Does the rating help to explain the character's behavior?

A SCALE OF STRESSES

This is a list of events that occur commonly in people's lives. The numbers in the column headed "Mean Value" indicate how stressful each event is. More specifically, a high number means the event is intensely stressful and will take a long time to adjust to.

Thinking about the last year, note the events that happened to you. By each event, indicate the number of times that it occurred in the past twelve months. Multiply this number, or frequency, by the number in the "Mean Value" column. Adding all of these products (event frequency × value) will give you your total stress score for the year. A total score of **150–199** indicates mild life crisis. **200–299**: moderate life crisis. **300 +** : major life crisis.

LIFE EVENT	MEAN VALUE			STRESS INDEX
Death of spouse	_____	×	100 =	_____
Divorce	_____	×	73 =	_____
Marital separation	_____	×	65 =	_____
Jail term	_____	×	63 =	_____
Death of close family member	_____	×	63 =	_____
Personal injury or illness	_____	×	53 =	_____
Marriage	_____	×	50 =	_____
Fired at work	_____	×	47 =	_____
Marital reconciliation	_____	×	45 =	_____
Retirement	_____	×	45 =	_____
Change in health of family member	_____	×	44 =	_____
Pregnancy	_____	×	40 =	_____
Sex difficulties	_____	×	39 =	_____
Gain of new family member	_____	×	39 =	_____
Business readjustment	_____	×	39 =	_____
Change in financial state	_____	×	38 =	_____
Death of close friend	_____	×	37 =	_____
Change to different line of work	_____	×	36 =	_____
Change in number of arguments with spouse	_____	×	35 =	_____
Mortgage over $10,000	_____	×	31 =	_____
Foreclosure of mortgage or loan	_____	×	30 =	_____
Change in responsibilities at work	_____	×	29 =	_____
Son or daughter leaving home	_____	×	29 =	_____
Trouble with in-laws	_____	×	29 =	_____
Outstanding personal achievement	_____	×	28 =	_____
Wife beginning or stopping work	_____	×	26 =	_____
Begin or end school	_____	×	26 =	_____
Change in living conditions	_____	×	25 =	_____
Revision of personal habits	_____	×	24 =	_____
Trouble with boss	_____	×	23 =	_____
Change in work hours or conditions	_____	×	20 =	_____
Change in residence	_____	×	20 =	_____
Change in schools	_____	×	20 =	_____

A SCALE OF STRESSES *continued*

LIFE EVENT	MEAN VALUE			STRESS INDEX
Change in recreation	_____ ×	19	=	_____
Change in church activities	_____ ×	19	=	_____
Change in social activities	_____ ×	18	=	_____
Mortgage or loan less than $10,000	_____ ×	17	=	_____
Change in sleeping habits	_____ ×	16	=	_____
Change in number of family get-togethers	_____ ×	15	=	_____
Change in eating habits	_____ ×	15	=	_____
Vacation	_____ ×	13	=	_____
Christmas	_____ ×	12	=	_____
Minor violations of the law	_____ ×	11	=	_____
	TOTAL		=	_____

[Now return to After Reading on page 145.]

HOW I READ IT

In your reading log, write about how you read the scale. Was it easy or hard? How long did it take you to figure out what to do? What helped you? Were you a slow or fast reader in this?

Share what you wrote with your group.

HOW IT'S WRITTEN

1. With your group, talk about how the stresses are arranged. What is the order? Why? Do you agree with the order? If not, which stresses do you think are out of order? Why? Which items on the list surprised you? Which items didn't surprise you? Why?

2. Where on the scale would you put "moving to a new culture" or "starting college"? What items are missing that you might like to add?

3. What does looking at the order of stresses tell you about writing? Write for a few minutes in your log.

TOPICS FOR WRITING

Choose one activity.

Activity A: Choose one of the stressful events you underwent this past year, and write the story of what happened. Tell it from beginning to end, giving as many details as you need to make it clear.

Activity B: All of the events on the list are common in people's lives. A person might wonder how such a common happening as starting a new school year, trouble with the boss, or getting married could be stressful. Choose one of events on the list that you are familiar with. Write about the situation, describing what happens to a person that makes it stressful. Use details that *show* us the stress.

Activity C: Choose one or two of the sentences you underlined in After Reading 2. Write a composition or a letter starting with the sentence you chose. You can explain them, agree or disagree with them based on your experience, or use them as advice to someone under stress.

AFTER WRITING

1. Read your piece aloud to your group. Ask group members to tell you what they understood and one thing that is not clear.

2. Choose the piece from your group that you think the class would like to hear, and ask a volunteer to read it aloud.

About All the Readings in This Chapter

PREPARING FOR WRITING

1. Reread all the entries in your reading log for this chapter.
   a. Write a list of issues you found in your reading log. Make a list of generalizations about those issues. (See p. 32 for an explanation of issues and generalizations.)
   b. Choose one generalization. Write it at the top of the page. List under it all the reasons and examples you can think of that prove it is true, including something you read in this chapter and something you wrote.

2. What is the relationship of stress, growth, and change? Does one cause another? Is stress necessary for growth and change to happen? Look through the readings. Think of your own life. Use one example from your own life and one from the readings to show the relationship of stress, growth, and change as you understand it. Discuss your examples with your group.

3. Look through the writing you have done for this chapter. Choose one piece that tells a story of something that happened to you or someone you know.

   Make a list of generalizations you could make about personal growth and change that you could support with one or more of the readings in this chapter.

TOPICS FOR WRITING

Choose one activity.

Activity A: Write a composition about your generalization. Try including an introduction in which you discuss an assumption some people have that you are going to disprove in your composition. For example, you could begin your first paragraph by saying, "Many young people believe that all changes take place in youth. They think that by the time we are 30 years old, we are fully formed. However, ..."

Activity B: Think of the turning points in your own life. Did they happen to you, or did you make them happen? Write a composition explaining your point of view.

Activity C: Choose a piece that you wrote for one of the readings in this chapter and revise it in light of what you have learned from the other readings in this chapter. Use what you wrote in Preparing for Writing 1 and 2 to guide you.

AFTER WRITING

1. Share what you wrote with your group. Ask group members to write down the main idea of your composition and then to list all the supporting information they can remember. Ask them to tell you other ways that you might make your point more powerfully.

2. Write in your log about *how* you wrote this composition. For example, how did you get ideas? Did the Preparing for Writing activities help you? How did you feel about rereading what you had written earlier in the chapter? Did your group's suggestions change the way you looked at your writing?

Extra Readings

What to Do About Stress

The following tips on how to respond to stress are taken from a flyer distributed to college students on a large urban campus.

WHAT TO DO?

You can't remove stress from you life but you can:

1. Change your perception of it.
2. Learn methods of controlling it.
3. Reduce the physical/mental effects of the stress response (a reaction that usually involves the release of adrenaline into the body).

Here Are Some Tips on How to Respond to Stress in Your Life:

1. Improve your diet to strengthen the immune system.

2. Increase physical exercise (endurance): Aerobic exercise helps reduce the negative effects of the "fight or flight" and chronic stress response.

3. Learn relaxation techniques to reduce stress, put your body back into a balanced state and help prevent further responses.

4. Learn methods to control stress such as time management, learning to say "no," and assertiveness.

5. Develop positive attitudes and belief systems.

Selections from *Imaginary Crimes*
Sheila Ballantyne

The following two excerpts are from Sheila Ballantyne's novel Imaginary Crimes, *the story of a girl growing up in the 1940s. In early adolescence, she loses her mother and continues growing to adulthood with her father and a younger sister.*

THE SHEIK

One Saturday while I was out swimming, Daddy found my copy of *The Sheik*. I had hidden it under my bed in the beginning, but as time went by I became sloppy and left it lying around in plain view.

When I came in the door, dripping stale lake water onto the peeling linoleum, he was standing in the kitchen with *The Sheik* on the counter, whipping himself up for what promised to be at least a three-quarter-of-an-hour job. "I want an explanation for THIS," he said, flicking his nails on the cover.

"Come," he whispered, his passionate eyes devouring her.
She fought against the fascination with which they dominated her, resisting him dumbly with tight-locked lips till he held her palpitating in his arms.

"Little fool," he said with a deepening smile. "Better me than my men."

"Oh, you brute! You brute!" she wailed, until his kisses silenced her.

"Did you hear what I said? I want an explanation why this cheap crap was in your room."

She became aware that night had fallen, and that they were still steadily galloping southward. In a few moments she was wide awake, and found that she was lying across the saddle in front of the Sheik, and that he was holding her in the crook of his arm. Her head was resting just over his heart, and she could feel the regular beat beneath her cheek. . . . With a start of recollection she realised fully whose arm was round her, and whose breast her head was resting on. Her heart beat with sudden violence. What was the matter with her? Why did she

"Look at me, you numbskull! Where the hell are your brains? Did you hear what I said?"

"No. What? What are you talking about?"

"Don't play dumb with me! I know trash when I see it, and this is trash! I try to teach you culture and refinement, and you . . .'"

not shrink from the pressure of his arm and the contact of his warm, strong body? What had happened to her? Quite suddenly she knew— knew that she loved him, that she had loved him for a long time, even when she thought she hated him and when she had fled from him. She knew now why his face had haunted her in the little oasis at midday— that it was love calling to her subconsciously.

"God damn it all to hell!" He was screaming now. I wrapped my towel more tightly around me. There was a huge puddle of water on the dark linoleum floor. My mind wasn't working at all; instead of racing wildly to manufacture some explanation, it simply dripped, like the water on the floor—aimless and liquid, a blank.

His dark, passionate eyes burnt into her like a hot flame. His encircling arms were like bands of fire, scorching her. His touch was torture. Helpless, like a trapped wild thing, she lay against him, panting, trembling, her wide eyes fixed on him, held against their will.

"It says right here, 'Seattle Public Library, due . . .' Jesus Christ Almighty, you've had this piece of shit out for over five months! Do you know what this is going to cost me in fines? Why, this is just like taking the food out of your little sister's mouth! Do you have any idea what opinion the librarian will have of you?"

> But she knew herself at last and knew the love that filled her, an overwhelming, passionate love that almost frightened her with its immensity and with the sudden hold it had laid upon her. Love had come to her at last who had scorned it so fiercely. The men who had loved her had not had the power to touch her, she had given love to no one, she had thought that she could not love, that she was devoid of all natural affection and that she would never know what love meant. But she knew now—a love of such complete surrender that she had never conceived. Her heart was given for all time to the fierce desert man who was so different from all other men whom she had met. . . .

"I have forbidden you to read this trash. I have tried to bring you up to appreciate the finer things of life, but all you read is cheap crap! *The Black Stallion! The Black Stallion Returns! The Son of the Black Stallion! The Island Stallion! The Roan Stallion!* Jesus P. Christ Almighty, and now, *The Sheik!*" He leaned on the counter and wiped his forehead with the back of his sleeve.

The Sheik was my turning point; it marked that place where I entered the world of adult passion, however removed, and self-assertion, however undignified. I grabbed the book off the counter and ran out of the house, shouting, "If you take *The Sheik* away you'll never see me again!" The neighbors turned off their hoses and stared. *The Sheik* was never mentioned again.

STRIPPING THE GEARS

Daddy taught me to drive the day I turned fifteen. We would all get in the Ford, Greta in the back seat and Daddy beside me, and head for the relative calm of Lake Washington Boulevard. It was hard learning to drive with Daddy screaming in the front seat and Greta screaming in the back. "Oh, Daddy, she's going in the lake! She's going in the lake! We're all going to die!"

"Take it easy, Greta; she's not going to do any such thing. No daughter of mine goes in the lake."

His confidence would carry me a few blocks until he, too, started screaming. "Look out! Look out! Watch it, watch it; Jesus Christ, you're stripping the gears!" It didn't take me long to learn that, to him, nothing was worse: cutting in front of another car; slicing into someone's neatly trimmed parking strip; going too near the edge of the lake—these were trivial, compared with stripping the gears.

"Let the clutch out *slowly!*" he would shout as we jerked along. I was sweating and frantic. I hated the lessons, but was determined to learn. I knew instinctively that driving would be my salvation in years to come.

It finally came together in spite of Daddy's efforts. If there was anything I learned from him that summer, it was how to strip the gears. When I finally got my license and was driving along the lake at midnight with my head out the window, singing along with the Top Ten, I stripped and stripped away at his shitty old gears. Nothing gave me greater pleasure; I was able to go to sleep without any trouble at all.

Becoming a Writer
Russell Baker

Growing Up, *Russell Baker's autobiographical account of his youth, includes this story of his early decision to become a writer.*

The notion of becoming a writer had flickered off and on in my head . . . but it wasn't until my third year in high school that the possibility took hold. Until then I'd been bored by everything associated with English courses. I found English grammar dull and baffling. I hated the assignments to turn out "compositions," and went at them like heavy labor, turning out laden, lackluster paragraphs that were agonies for teachers to read and for me to write. The classics thrust on me to read seemed as deadening as chloroform.

When our class was assigned to Mr. Fleagle for third-year English I anticipated another grim year in that dreariest of subjects. Mr. Fleagle was notorious among City students for dullness and inability to inspire. He was said to be stuffy, dull, and hopelessly out of date. To me he looked to be sixty or seventy and prim to a fault. He wore primly severe eyeglasses, his wavy hair was primly cut and primly combed. He wore prim vested suits with neckties blocked primly against the collar buttons of his primly starched white shirts. He had a primly pointed jaw, a primly straight nose, and prim manner of speaking that was so correct, so gentlemanly, that he seemed a comic antique.

I anticipated a listless, unfruitful year with Mr. Fleagle and for a long time was not disappointed. We read *Macbeth*. Mr. Fleagle loved *Macbeth* and wanted us to love it too, but he lacked the gift of infecting others with his own passion. He tried to convey the murderous ferocity of Lady Macbeth one day by reading aloud the passage that concludes

. . . I have given suck, and know
How tender 'tis to love the babe that milks me.
I would, while it was smiling in my face,
Have plucked my nipple from his boneless gums.. . . .

The idea of prim Mr. Fleagle plucking his nipple from boneless gums was too much for the class. We burst into gasps of irrepressible snickering. Mr. Fleagle stopped.

"There is nothing funny, boys, about giving suck to a babe. It is the—the very essence of motherhood, don't you see."

He constantly sprinkled his sentences with "don't you see." It wasn't a question but an exclamation of mild surprise at our ignorance. "Your pronoun needs an antecedent, don't you see," he would say, very primly. "The purpose of the Porter's scene, boys, is to provide comic relief from the horror, don't you see."

Late in the year we tackled the informal essay. "The essay, don't you see, is the . . ." My mind went numb. Of all forms of writing, none seemed so boring as the essay. Naturally we would have to write informal essays. Mr. Fleagle distributed a homework sheet offering us a choice of topics. None was quite so simpleminded as "What I Did on My Summer Vacation," but most seemed to be almost as dull. I took the list home and dawdled until the night before the essay was due. Sprawled on the sofa, I finally faced up to the grim task, took the list out of my notebook, and scanned it. The topic on which my eye stopped was "The Art of Eating Spaghetti."

This title produced an extraordinary sequence of mental images. Surging up to the depths of memory came a vivid recollection of a night in Belleville when all of us were seated around the supper table—Uncle Allen, my mother, Uncle Charlie, Doris, Uncle Hal—and Aunt Pat served spaghetti for supper. Spaghetti was an exotic treat in those days. Neither Doris nor I had ever eaten spaghetti, and none of the adults had enough experience to be good at it. All the good humor of Uncle Allen's house reawoke in my mind as I recalled the laughing arguments we had that night about the socially respectable method for moving spaghetti from plate to mouth.

Suddenly I wanted to write about that, about the warmth and good feeling of it, but I wanted to put it down simply for my own joy, not for Mr. Fleagle. It was a moment I wanted to recapture and hold for myself. I wanted to relive the pleasure of an evening at New Street. To write it as I wanted, however, would violate all the rules of formal composition I'd learned in school, and Mr. Fleagle would surely give it a failing grade. Never mind. I would write something else for Mr. Fleagle after I had written this thing for myself.

When I finished it the night was half gone and there was no time left to compose a proper, respectable essay for Mr. Fleagle. There was no choice next morning but to turn in my private reminiscence of Belleville. Two days passed before Mr. Fleagle returned the graded papers, and he returned everyone's but mine. I was bracing myself for a command to report to Mr. Fleagle immediately after school for discipline when I saw him lift my paper from his desk and rap for the class's attention.

"Now, boys," he said, "I want to read you an essay. This is titled 'The Art of Eating Spaghetti.'"

And he started to read. My words! He was reading *my words* out loud to the entire class. What's more, the entire class was listening. Listening attentively. Then somebody laughed, then the entire class was laughing, and not in contempt and ridicule, but with openhearted enjoyment. Even Mr. Fleagle stopped two or three times to repress a small prim smile.

I did my best to avoid showing pleasure, but what I was feeling was pure ecstasy at this startling demonstration that my words had the power to make people laugh. In the eleventh grade, at the eleventh hour as it were, I had discovered a calling. It was the happiest moment of my entire school career. When Mr. Fleagle finished he put the final seal on my happiness by saying, "Now that, boys, is an essay, don't you see. It's—don't you see—it's of the very essence of the essay, don't you see. Congratulations, Mr. Baker."

For the first time, light shone on a possibility. It wasn't a very heartening possibility, to be sure. Writing couldn't lead to a job after high school, and it was hardly honest work, but Mr. Fleagle had opened a door for me. After that I ranked Mr. Fleagle among the finest teachers in the school.

Everything Stuck to Him
Raymond Carver

This short story appeared in a collection of stories by Raymond Carver, What We Talk about When We Talk about Love.

She's in Milan for Christmas and wants to know what it was like when she was a kid.

Tell me, she says. Tell me what it was like when I was a kid. She sips Strega, waits, eyes him closely.

She is a cool, slim, attractive girl, a survivor from top to bottom.

That was a long time ago. That was twenty years ago, he says.

You can remember, she says. Go on.

What do you want to hear? he says. What else can I tell you? I could tell you about something that happened when you were a baby. It involves you, he says. But only in a minor way.

Tell me, she says. But first fix us another so you won't have to stop in the middle.

He comes back from the kitchen with drinks, settles into his chair, begins.

They were kids themselves, but they were crazy in love, this eighteen-year-old boy and this seventeen-year-old girl when they married. Not all that long afterwards they had a daughter.

The baby came along in late November during a cold spell that just happened to coincide with the peak of the waterfowl season. The boy loved to hunt, you see. That's part of it.

The boy and girl, husband and wife, father and mother, they lived in a little apartment under a dentist's office. Each night they cleaned the dentist's place upstairs in exchange for rent and utilities. In summer they were expected to maintain the lawn and the flowers. In winter the boy shoveled snow and spread rock salt on the walks. Are you still with me? Are you getting the picture?

I am, she says.

That's good, he says. So one day the dentist finds out they were using his letterhead for their personal correspondence. But that's another story.

He gets up from his chair and looks out the window. He sees the tile rooftops and the snow that is falling steadily on them.

Tell the story, she says.

The two kids were very much in love. On top of this they had great ambitions. They were always talking about the things they were going to do and the places they were going to go.

Now the boy and girl slept in the bedroom, and the baby slept in the living room. Let's say the baby was about three months old and had only just begun to sleep through the night.

On this one Saturday night after finishing his work upstairs, the boy stayed in the dentist's office and called an old hunting friend of his father's.

Carl, he said when the man picked up the receiver, believe it or not, I'm a father.

Congratulations, Carl said. How is the wife?

She's fine, Carl. Everybody's fine.

That's good, Carl said, I'm glad to hear it. But if you called about going hunting, I'll tell you something. The geese are flying to beat the band. I don't think I've ever seen so many. Got five today. Going back in the morning, so come along if you want to.

I want to, the boy said.

The boy hung up the telephone and went downstairs to tell the girl. She watched while he laid out his things. Hunting coat, shell bag, boots, socks, hunting cap, long underwear, pump gun.

What time will you be back? the girl said.

Probably around noon, the boy said. But maybe as late as six o'clock. Would that be too late?

It's fine, she said. The baby and I will get along fine. You go and have some fun. When you get back, we'll dress the baby up and go visit Sally.

The boy said, Sounds like a good idea.

Sally was the girl's sister. She was striking. I don't know if you've seen pictures of her. The boy was a little in love with Sally, just as he was a little in love with Betsy, who was another sister the girl had. The boy used to say to the girl, If we weren't married, I could go for Sally.

What about Betsy? the girl used to say. I hate to admit it, but I truly feel she's better looking than Sally and me. What about Betsy?

Betsy too, the boy used to say.

After dinner he turned up the furnace and helped her bathe the baby. He marveled again at the infant who had half his features and half the girl's. He powdered the tiny body. He powdered between fingers and toes.

He emptied the bath into the sink and went upstairs to check the air. It was overcast and cold. The grass, what there was of it, looked like canvas, stiff and gray under the street light.

Snow lay in piles beside the walk. A car went by. He heard sand under the tires. He let himself imagine what it might be like tomorrow, geese beating the air over his head, shotgun plunging against his shoulder.

Then he locked the door and went downstairs.

In bed they tried to read. But both of them fell asleep, she first, letting the magazine sink to the quilt.

It was the baby's cries that woke him up.

The light was on out there, and the girl was standing next to the crib rocking the baby in her arms. She put the baby down, turned out the light, and came back to the bed.

He heard the baby cry. This time the girl stayed where she was. The baby cried fitfully and stopped. The boy listened, then dozed. But the baby's cries woke him again. The living room light was burning. He sat up and turned on the lamp.

I don't know what's wrong, the girl said, walking back and forth with the baby. I've changed her and fed her, but she keeps on crying. I'm so tired I'm afraid I might drop her.

You come back to bed, the boy said. I'll hold her for a while.

He got up and took the baby, and the girl went to lie down again.

Just rock her for a few minutes, the girl said from the bedroom. Maybe she'll go back to sleep.

The boy sat on the sofa and held the baby. He jiggled it in his lap until he got its eyes to close, his own eyes closing right along. He rose carefully and put the baby back in the crib.

It was a quarter to four, which gave him forty-five minutes. He crawled into bed and dropped off. But a few minutes later the baby was crying again, and this time they both got up.

The boy did a terrible thing. He swore.

For God's sake, what's the matter with you? the girl said to the boy. Maybe she's sick or something. Maybe we shouldn't have given her the bath.

The boy picked up the baby. The baby kicked its feet and smiled.

Look, the boy said, I really don't think there's anything wrong with her.

How do you know that? the girl said. Here, let me have her. I know I ought to give her something, but I don't know what it's supposed to be.

The girl put the baby down again. The boy and the girl looked at the baby, and the baby began to cry.

The girl took the baby. Baby, baby, the girl said with tears in her eyes.

Probably it's something on her stomach, the boy said.

The girl didn't answer. She went on rocking the baby, paying no attention to the boy.

The boy waited. He went to the kitchen and put on water for coffee. He drew his woolen underwear on over his shorts and T-shirt, buttoned up, then got into his clothes.

What are you doing? the girl said.

Going hunting, the boy said.

I don't think you should, she said. I don't want to be left alone with her like this.

Carl's planning on me going, the boy said. We've planned it.

I don't care about what you and Carl planned, she said. And I don't care about Carl, either. I don't even know Carl.

You've met Carl before. You know him, the boy said. What do you mean you don't know him?

That's not the point and you know it, the girl said.

What is the point? the boy said. The point is we planned it.

The girl said, I'm your wife. This is your baby. She's sick or something. Look at her. Why else is she crying?

I know you're my wife, the boy said.

The girl began to cry. She put the baby back in the crib. But the baby started up again. The girl dried her eyes on the sleeve of her nightgown and picked the baby up.

The boy laced up his boots. He put on his shirt, his sweater, his coat. The kettle whistled on the stove in the kitchen.

You're going to have to choose, the girl said. Carl or us. I mean it.

What do you mean? the boy said.

You heard what I said, the girl said. If you want a family, you're going to have to choose.

They stared at each other. Then the boy took up his hunting gear and went outside. He started the car. He went around to the car windows and, making a job of it, scraped away the ice.

He turned off the motor and sat awhile. And then he got out and went back inside.

The living-room light was on. The girl was asleep on the bed. The baby was asleep beside her.

The boy took off his boots. Then he took off everything else. In his socks and his long underwear, he sat on the sofa and read the Sunday paper.

The girl and the baby slept on. After a while, the boy went to the kitchen and started frying bacon.

The girl came out in her robe and put her arms around the boy.

Hey, the boy said.

I'm sorry, the girl said.

It's all right, the boy said.

I didn't mean to snap like that.

It was my fault, he said.

You sit down, the girl said. How does a waffle sound with bacon?

Sounds great, the boy said.

She took the bacon out of the pan and made waffle batter. He sat at the table and watched her move around the kitchen.

She put a plate in front of him with bacon, a waffle. He spread butter and poured syrup. But when he started to cut, he turned the plate into his lap.

I don't believe it, he said, jumping up from the table.

If you could see yourself, the girl said.

The boy looked down at himself, at everything stuck to his underwear.

I was starved, he said, shaking his head.

You were starved, she said, laughing.

He peeled off the woolen underwear and threw it at the bathroom door. Then he opened his arms and the girl moved into them.

We won't fight anymore, she said.

The boy said, We won't.

He gets up from his chair and refills their glasses.

That's it, he says. End of story. I admit it's not much of a story.

I was interested, she says.

He shrugs and carries his drink over to the window. It's dark now but still snowing.

Things change, he says. I don't know how they do. But they do without your realizing it or wanting them to.

Yes that's true, only—But she does not finish what she started.

She drops the subject. In the window's reflection he sees her study her nails. Then she raises her head. Speaking brightly, she asks if he is going to show her the city, after all.

He says, Put your boots on and let's go.

But he stays by the window, remembering. They had laughed. They had leaned on each other and laughed until the tears had come, while everything else—the cold, and where he'd go in it—was outside, for a while anyway.

Chapter 5

Change and Resisting Change

1. Read the title of the chapter. Freewrite for a few minutes in your reading log about those words.

2. Share what you wrote with a partner. Write down one connection between what you wrote and what your partner wrote.

BEFORE READING

1. The title of this poem is "First Grade." What do you call the first year of formal schooling in your culture? Freewrite for a few minutes about how you feel when you hear this term.

2. Read the introductory information. Discuss it with your group.

3. Read "First Grade."

First Grade
Phil George

Phil George is a Native American of the Nez Percé–Tsimshian tribe. He has written in another poem that he was given his name, Phil George, by a teacher who must have found his Indian name, Two Swans Ascending from Still Waters, too difficult to remember.

From moccasins* to shoes—
    Unsteady steps,
Unwilling to unlearn
    Old Ways.

AFTER READING

1. How does this poem make you feel? Write a response in your reading log.

2. Phil George says that his steps were "Unwilling to unlearn Old Ways." With a partner, decide what you think he means by this, and then make a list of things the two of you might not want to unlearn. Share your list with your group. Make a group list.

3. Choose three or four items that you find particularly interesting on your group's "unwilling to unlearn" list, and report them to the whole class. Make a class list on the board and discuss it.

---

*Moccasins are soft deerskin shoes traditionally worn by many Native Americans.

HOW IT'S WRITTEN

Often, books about correct writing in English recommend putting statements in positive form. It is better, these books suggest, to say "He usually came late" than to say "He was not often on time." Talk to your group about why Phil George used three negative words, *unsteady*, *unwilling*, and *unlearn*, in his short poem.

TOPICS FOR WRITING

Choose one activity.

Activity A: Think of a piece of clothing or another object associated with one particular stage of life (such as diapers) or a particular culture. Write a poem or a paragraph in which you use that piece of clothing or object to symbolize a transition someone has made in life, as Phil George does with moccasins.

Activity B: Write a paragraph or a poem called "First Grade" (or the corresponding term in your language) in which you describe one major change people from your tradition must make when they enter school.

Activity C: Look back at the lists you made in After Reading 3. Choose one item on the list. Imagine readers who think you should unlearn it. Write a composition using strong reasons and examples to persuade them that they are wrong.

AFTER WRITING

1. Share your writing with your group.
2. As a group, choose the piece you like best, and have it read aloud to the whole class.

BEFORE READING

1. Read the title and introductory information about the passage.

2. Write down a question you would like to be answered in the passage. Share your question with your group, and make a group list of questions.

3. With the class and instructor, write on the chalkboard the words you associate with the word *macho*. With a partner, put the words into categories, and give each category a heading (title).

4. Read the selection.

Taming Macho Ways
Elvia Alvarado

This selection is taken from the true story of Elvia Alvarado, who worked as an organizer of the peasant women in her community in Honduras for the National Congress of Rural Workers (CNTC). In the process, she evolved from passively accepting her poverty-stricken life to actively changing the conditions of her life and community. In this passage, she talks about wanting to change the way men and women treat each other.

Machismo is a historical problem. It goes back to the time of our great-grandfathers, or our great-great-grandfathers. In my mind, it's connected to the problem of drinking. Drinking is man's worst disease. When men drink, they fight with everyone. They hit their wives and children. They offend their neighbors. They lose all sense of dignity.

How are we going to stop campesinos from drinking? First of all, we know the government isn't interested in stopping it, because it's an important source of income. Every time you buy a bottle of liquor, part of that money goes to the government.

That's why the government doesn't let the campesinos make their own liquor, because the government doesn't make any money off homemade brew. So a campesino can go into town any time, day or night, spend all his money, and drink himself sick. But if he gets caught making *choruco*—that's what we call homemade spirits made from corn and sugar—they throw him in jail. The government wants the campesinos to drink, but only the liquor that they make money off of.

If we're ever going to get campesinos to stop drinking, we first have to look at why so many campesinos drink. And for that we have to look at what kind of society we have. We've built up a society that treats people like trash, a society that doesn't give people jobs, a society that doesn't give people a reason to stay sober. I think that's where this vice comes from.

I've seen what happens when campesinos organize and have a plot of land to farm. They don't have time for drinking any more, except on special occasions. They spend the day in the hot sun—plowing, planting, weeding, irrigating, cutting firewood for the house, carrying the produce to market. Most of them are very dedicated to their work and their families.

So I've noticed that once the campesinos have a purpose, once they have a way to make a living and take care of their families, they drink less. And they usually stop beating their wives, too. And I've seen that once the women get organized, they start to get their husbands in line.

I know that changing the way men and women treat each other is a long process. But if we really want to build a new society, we have to change the bad habits of the past. We can't build a new society if we are drunks, womanizers, or corrupt. No, those things have to change.

But people *can* change. I know there are many things I used to do that I don't do any more, now that I'm more educated. For example, I used to gossip and criticize other women. I used to fight over men. But I learned that gossip only destroys, it doesn't build. Criticizing my neighbors doesn't create unity. Neither does fighting over men. So I stopped doing these things.

Before, whenever I'd see the slightest thing I'd go running to my friends, "Ay, did you see so-and-so with what's-his-face?" I'd go all over town telling everyone what I saw. Now I could see a woman screwing a man in the middle of the street and I wouldn't say anything. That's her business.

If someone is in danger, then, yes, we have to get involved. For example, I heard a rumor that a landowner was out to kill one of the campesino leaders I work with. I made sure to warn the campesino so he'd be careful. That kind of rumor we tell each other—but not idle gossip.

I also used to flirt with married men, just for the fun of it and to make their wives jealous. Now I'm much more responsible, much more serious. That doesn't mean I don't joke around and have a good time. I just make it clear that we're friends.

We all have to make changes. Campesino men have to be more responsible with their women. They have to have only one woman. Because they have a hard enough time supporting one family, let alone two. Campesinos who drink have to stop drinking. And campesinos who fight with their wives have to stop fighting. Our struggle has to begin in our own homes.

AFTER READING

1. Write for a few minutes in your log what you understand the passage is about and how you feel about it. Read over what you wrote, and underline the sentences that best express what you think and feel. Save this for discussion with your group.

2. As a group, look at the list of questions your group made before reading. Which can be answered by the passage? Find the sentences or paragraphs in the text that would contribute to the answer. Mark those places with the question number (1, 2, etc.).

   Then write another set of questions you and your group still have.

3. Choose one activity.

   Activity A: If you aren't familiar with Spanish, first write down possible definitions of *machismo* and *campesino*. Then find out the meaning of those words from a native speaker of Spanish in the class (or a dictionary). Refine your definition.

   Activity B: The author, Elvia Alvarado, says "people *can* change" and uses herself as an example: "There are many things I used to do that I don't do any more, now that I'm more educated." With a partner, make a list of specific ways in which people change when they become more educated.

4. Report your findings to your group.

TOPICS FOR WRITING

Choose one activity.

Activity A: Most societies have traditionally been dominated by men. But many societies have changed, and women now have equal rights. Still, even in societies where men and women are considered equal, some traditions, behaviors, and patterns of unequal treatment persist. Write about some of the changes in your society and about any inequalities that persist.

Activity B: Alvarado talks about the relationship between machismo and drinking alcohol. She sees them as connected. In your experience and observations, is there a connection between drinking and male dominance? What are the traditions and customs in your culture about drinking? Is drinking usually associated with men? Who drinks, where, when, and how? Write an essay, giving examples where possible.

Activity C: Choose a sentence or paragraph from the passage that is meaningful to you. It may be an issue or topic that makes you angry or that you have experience with. Write an essay about it, telling how the issue or topic comes up in Alvarado's story and then how it relates to you. Look back at your log for ideas.

AFTER WRITING

1. Form a group with two or three other people in the class who wrote on the same topic you did. Read your papers aloud to one another. Notice the different ways in which you approached the same topic. Make a list of the differences and similarities in your papers.

2. Report to the whole class on what your group wrote about, giving a one- or two-sentence summary of each person's ideas on the topic, differences, and similarities.

BEFORE READING
---

1. The word *spirit* has several meanings. What do you think of when you hear the word? Freewrite for 3 minutes in your reading log about it.

    Share what you wrote with a partner. Discuss any similarities and differences in what you wrote.

2. Read the title and introductory information. Do you expect any of the meanings of the word *spirit* that you wrote down in Before Reading 1 to appear in the piece? If so, tell your partner which ones.

Eskimo Women Spirits
Robert Coles and Jane Hallowell Coles

This excerpt is taken from the book Women in Crisis *by Robert Coles and Jane Hallowell Coles, which is about five poor and uneducated but remarkable American women. This story is about "Lorna," an Alaskan Eskimo woman given her name by the wife of a missionary. Lorna resists the influence of the "Lower Forty-Eight" (that is, the rest of the continental United States) and makes major changes in her small Eskimo village.*

The Arctic wind takes possession of her, she claims. For brief spells she is no longer herself. She stands still, closes her eyes, lets her self rise, spread across the tundra, then fade away—the return to her body. She loves leaving, loves coming back. Her eyes see the wind approaching: the aroused waves; the grass bending; the birds tossing, riding their way on the currents, holding to a course. Her eyes contemplate the return of her "spirit": quiet water, a gentle flat land, a new stillness to the air. . . .

She was, as a child, her own kind of person. At seven, eight, or nine she had among the villagers a secure reputation as an especially sturdy, independent, self-reliant, and imaginative child who stuck close to her father and helped him more and more in the course of his various duties. In school, however, she was regarded as "strange" by the Anglo teacher, a young man who had chosen to volunteer his Christian energy and sensibility to the settlement's missionary church, and had found teaching the best way to do so. The church's missionary minister also regarded young Lorna as "strange." Once he told her father that she was a "tomboy." The father smiled, asked for a clarification. The minister observed that the girl spent most of her time with the father, or with some younger boys in the village, whom she seemed mostly to boss. The father continued to smile, but said nothing. Later, he talked with his daughter about the company she kept. The girl, then nine, had heard similar comments from others. She had her explanation—that she liked her father and wanted to stay with him as much as possible, and that a few boys admired her father for his magical abilities as a repairman, and admired her for being of so much help to him.

As a grown woman, she still remembered a speech of sorts she gave at school when she was asked what she wanted to do later in life: "I told the teacher that I didn't know what I'd be doing when I'm bigger. I told the teacher that I might turn into a caribou, and run away, and never come near the village. I might become a polar bear, and watch our village from some ice out in the harbor. The teacher didn't like the way I was talking! But I didn't like the way the teacher was talking! The teachers who come here usually stay for two or three years. They want us to think just as they do. They tell our children to dream of airplanes and submarines and snowmobiles and radios and hi-fi sets and television. They tell our children to go to school in the cities or down in the Lower Forty-Eight, and to live there because there's nothing to do here but get through one season and then another. My father used to squeeze my hand when a season was ending, and say that we'd won a victory, and now we'd better get ready for a new struggle. But the minister thought my father wasn't enough of a Christian. The minister always gave God the credit for what we, the Eskimos, did—but he boasted about all the things the United States has done. If one of us took medicine, it wasn't God's; it was from a doctor or a hospital: the white man. . . .

"Some Eskimos don't learn from the right visitors. They pay attention to the white people who come here, but not to the geese. They listen to the honk of the ministers and teachers who come here, and to the honk of the machines, but not to the geese. . . . A goose won't go just anywhere. A goose chooses the right place, to suit it. The Eskimo sometimes does what the white people think is right; the Eskimo doesn't decide what is right—for the Eskimo. My father says that we should be ourselves and no one else.

"I don't even care what my brothers say, or my friends and cousins—not when I'm working with my father. He and I have been building a house, and my cousins have asked why I'm doing it with him. I'm a girl, they tell me. They are girls, and they are reminding me that I'm a girl! I thank them! I tell them that it's a good thing they told me I'm a girl, because if they hadn't I wouldn't know. Finally, I asked them where they got their idea of what I should do and what I shouldn't do. They went to school, they remind me. They listened to the teachers. They go to church; they listen to the minister. I am supposed to be grateful that they know so much. They sure know what to tell me! They think I should sit and smile and wait for one of their brothers to come and ask me for a ride in the snowmobile. They think I should be dreaming of the five or ten children I'll have one day. They think that I should be cooking with my mother, not telling her good-bye, and going out to stand beside my father and try to help him. I'm too 'restless,' a teacher once told them, when she saw I wasn't near enough to hear." . . .

"My father wonders about children: will I have them? Yes—but I am waiting to meet the man who will stand up and be a strong Eskimo wind. He will blow away that store, with its bribes from the Lower Forty-Eight. I remember when we learned the word 'bribe' in school. We were being 'prepared,' like the teachers say, for 'the new Alaska.' If you're going to be bribed, you should know what's happening to you! When a bird is bribed, it can fly away and forget what happened. Not us; we stay, and wait and wait for more bribes. I've fed birds, but they leave right away. I suppose I could keep feeding them, and they'd stay. Would they be the birds we know? My father says the wind would take over—send them south, get them away from our bribes. Where is the wind to rescue us?"

A wind came to rescue her when she was eighteen—a cousin of hers. . . .

"I told Fred that he'd have to hear about me all his life, if we got married. I told him that I've become myself, and he's become himself, and I might end up taking him from himself—because his friends would say he should make me be like their wives, and I will never agree to give up being myself, and so there might be trouble. But he said no, I should stop being 'impatient'—with him! He said he knew what I'm like when he began to notice me and like me and follow me with his eyes. He went to talk with my father before he ever told me how much he likes me. He told my father first! He asked him if I would mind a husband who didn't try to make me into one of the village's 'regular wives.' My father knew what he meant. He told Fred that I can cook if I want to, but I won't cook just because everyone else thinks I should. Fred told him he liked to hear that about me. Then he told me, when we had our long talk, that he hoped I never gave in to anyone— including himself! I wanted to give in right then, and tell him I was ready to do anything he wanted! If he thought I'd make a 'patient' cook, I'd become one. We've joked ever since about my cooking. I don't do the best job; he is very helpful, and he usually finishes the cooking. I always start out, though. I get 'impatient' in the middle. I'll get to staring out the window or up the ceiling, and he will come up beside me and take over! Then I go feed the dogs or make sure the house doesn't need some work done."

They were married quietly, with only their immediate families in the church. . . .

One day . . . she happened to be near the village's landing strip, and saw some of her fellow villagers waiting for the plane to arrive—the weekly intermediary between them and the outside world. She, too, wanted to see the landing, and did. But she saw more. She saw the men on the plane talk with the men on the ground. She saw the women there withdraw, become a huddled group of expectant, attentive, quite respectful and certainly demure individuals. They occasionally giggled, but were mostly serious, even grave. The men, from the plane or the village, were a contrast indeed. They were open, expansive, friendly. They were enjoying the company of each other. They kidded. They even played a few games: who can throw a piece of wood farthest, or who can reach highest—various points on the plane being a measure of achievement.

Lorna knew that she wasn't *only* angry; she was frustrated, envious. She liked to throw—almost always by herself. She also liked to show how strong she is, how able to exert her muscles, her will, and thereby [exceed] even her own expectations. And she had learned to appreciate the airplane as extraordinarily valuable—a means by which one can leave a village and, only hours later, be standing far away on a relatively crowded city sidewalk. Why weren't the women near the plane? Why hadn't they shown an interest in it? Why were only men going in and out of the plane, loading and unloading? She suddenly remembered the harsh comments she had heard from her friend Sally in the Fairbanks airport—to the effect that men run everything from airplanes to businesses to governments. What would Sally say about this particular Eskimo village? Lorna asked herself that question as she stared at a rather ordinary event. She would never stop asking that question, nor would she keep her thoughts to herself, as had often been the case before.

She broke her own meditative gaze after about five minutes, and walked over to the plane. She made a point of passing the women. She asked them if they wanted to accompany her, catch a nearer look at the plane, even go aboard. They were stunned by her sudden appearance, her summons of sorts. . . . They kept their eyes on her. She knew she had a certain control over them as she walked toward the plane. She wasn't sure what she would do, once at her destination. She walked fast, arrived at the plane with one purpose in mind—to mingle with the others, and doing so, show the onlookers what might be possible for them. When she came near the village's men, they frowned at her: Lorna, up to her old tricks. She was always a bit unpredictable, and certainly a known maverick. But she usually confined her iconoclastic behavior to the tundra or the ocean's edge, where she walked, talked to herself, seemed caught in moods that defied anyone's comprehension. Now she was turning herself into a public figure, and seemingly challenging a long-standing social custom—the way a particular Eskimo settlement comes to terms with outsiders.

For a moment or two the men glared at her, but said nothing. She walked past them, ready to look at the plane, then board it for a closer inspection. She stopped just short of the steps leading to the inside of the plane. One of the Eskimo men, an old friend of her husband's, approached her and asked her what she wanted. She looked at him intently, more curious than angry (so she later described herself). Why should he be asking her what she wanted? Why wasn't she asking him, in response, what *he* was doing—asking her what she wanted? She said nothing in reply. But she was deterred by the question. She had intended to go up the stairs, poke around a bit, return to the ground, and leave for the tundra and a good, long walk. Now she had other plans in mind.

She started up the stairs, turned around, looked across the field to the women, who were, as she had suspected, still watching her every move. She raised both her arms and with them beckoned the women. They were, for a second, puzzled and unresponsive. But soon Lorna was calling to them: Come here, come and see, come right away. They had rarely heard her speak at all, never mind approach them directly and invitingly. They were as much surprised by the sound of her voice and the phenomenon of her willingness to engage with them, pay them heed, as they were with the message. They responded to *her*, not to her more ideological interest on their behalf. They walked nearer, eventually were beside her. Lorna, for her part, brushed aside years of her own indifference, if not outright hostility, and smiled, even touched the shoulders of several women. Then she casually suggested that they all go up and look at the inside of the airplane.

She spoke in such a way that she was not really asking anything special of her newfound friends. She simply started up the steps. The other women seemed to sense that if they did not follow, they would be breaking a fragile bond, suddenly, surprisingly established. Up they went, oblivious of the men, who now had come together and were watching this development with surprise rather than annoyance. They were, in fact, an image of the group of women as it had existed until a few minutes earlier; that is, they were outsiders, if nearer at hand, and they were quite obviously interested in what would happen *next*, even as the women had hitherto stood patiently and wondered what they would see from minute to minute, as the plane's crew went through various rituals.

Soon enough the women had, for the first time, obtained a rather thorough view of the plane's interior. They had also met the crew, been shown the controls, even been allowed to sit, one after the other, in the pilot's seat. Each of them was permitted to use a pair of binoculars. They were given a brief lecture on distances: how many miles to various points in Alaska, and to the south. Then they descended, looking rather pleased with themselves and, of course, excited. The men broke out of their group, rushed to the women, embraced them, and started clapping at them: congratulations! They walked together back to the village, the first time that had happened. Always before the arrival of a plane had been an occasion for the sexes to separate and keep apart, until both the men and the women had returned to their homes or adjacent land, and the plane could be seen high in the sky, circling, or only be heard.

Lorna did not realize the significance of the occasion at first: "I was almost in tears, but I didn't know why. It was the first time I'd ever felt friendly with those women. I used to avoid them whenever possible. And I knew what they thought of me: the strange one, the proud one, the one no one knows how to figure out! I'd heard the minister's complaints about me years ago, and tried to forget them. I thought of the minister when I was walking back from the landing strip with my new friends. He is gone. We have a new minister. I wished that the old one was there. I wondered what he'd make of it—all of us walking together, the men and the women. He always gave us sermons about men having *their* work, and women having *their* work. It used to bother him that my grandfather liked to cook and would teach some boys how to prepare a soup. He'd learned how to make it from a white man, a hunter, but that didn't make any difference to the minister. He thought that my grandfather shouldn't cook; my grandmother should do that. No wonder my grandfather would leave and walk toward the ocean when the minister came to our house for one of his visits.

"When we came back to our village, we just stood there. We didn't seem to want to break up and go back to our houses. I got nervous for a second. I didn't know what to say, or do. I decided to say nothing, and do nothing. We just talked a little about the plane. Then I saw that everyone felt a little funny, so I spoke up. I said that now we should all go to the plane *together* each week, and have a good time there on the landing strip *together*, and then come back here *together*. Everyone laughed and said yes. Then we all hugged—and that was the end. We went home. I was quite excited, but I didn't really know why. I didn't know, then, what had happened—or what would happen."

She attributed her excitement, at first, to a more personal matter—her reconciliation, of a kind, with the people of the village. But they had not missed the point of her involvement in their lives. They began to realize that she had, in her own quiet but forceful way, asked them to make a break with their past. They got to thinking about not only Lorna's initiative, but their response—and its justification: "I heard from Fred, day after day, that I had turned into a different Lorna, and that probably another spirit had taken me over. That wasn't what happened, though. I'm still the same person I was. It's the people of the village who began to change a little. They really look forward to that plane coming; they have a party there now at the landing strip. They bring Cokes, and they all go together. The women love looking inside the plane. I take Sally with me; and Fred comes when he isn't fishing. Sally told me that she would like to be a pilot. She told the schoolteacher, too; and the schoolteacher didn't like the idea. She told my daughter to be more 'realistic.' My daughter didn't know what the word means, and I wasn't sure either. We found out: you're being 'realistic' when you do what the teacher tells you to do! When you think something she doesn't like you to think, you're not being 'realistic' at all! I hope Sally doesn't worry all the time about the opinion of others, even when it's me who's telling her to do something, and she wants to do something else. I hope she does become a pilot! I'd love to be one myself!"

She would never stop having thoughts about being a pilot. That was her inclination, her way—to have dreams of departure, travel; dreams in which she goes away, does the unusual, the difficult, the unconventional; dreams, it might be said by others, of transcendence. All her life she had been dissatisfied with the constraints, as she saw them, of her village's everyday life. All her life she had regarded herself (and been regarded as) a somewhat different person—elusive, strange, aloof, self-preoccupied, imaginative to the point of eccentricity in her wishes, ambitions, even activities. She would never become just another Eskimo villager. But after the incident at the landing strip she did change slightly, and her husband and children and relatives and neighbors noticed the change. She went with the others quite eagerly to await the plane's arrival. She laughed and joked while standing there, and often, when the plane first appeared, she clapped loudly, prompting others to follow suit. Eventually she became, by common consent, the group's leader—in the sense that she went aboard first and greeted the pilot. Later on, she was the one to say good-bye to him, on behalf of all present.

One day, when Lorna was thirty-five years old, a pilot took her and her daughter Sally up on a flight, showed them how to use the controls—as opposed to looking at them. The village from that time on regarded both mother and daughter as pilots, no matter how hard both protested the mere beginning of their experience. When Lorna came back home from that flight she predicted that Sally would surely one day become a pilot, and that she would, perhaps, get to fly with her daughter upon occassion. The mother also announced to her family that many "Eskimo women spirits," long silent, had begun to speak up. Those spirits were responsible for the slow but definite changes taking place in the village—the mixed group at the landing strip, the more casual mingling of men and women at the village store. When Sally asked her mother whether more "spirits" would arrive, and what changes they would bring, the answer provided was prompt and brief: "I hope more spirits will come; I hope they will help all the women of this village fly."

AFTER READING

1. How was the word *spirit* used in this piece? Was it the same as the way you expected or different? Freewrite in your log for a few minutes about Lorna and the word *spirit*. Share your thoughts with a partner.

2. Work with a partner. Draw a horizontal line across a page in your reading log. This will be a time line along which you will chronologically mark all the events in Lorna's story. Go back through the text and discuss each event you are going to place on your line before you mark it.

3. Make a list of adjectives that describe Lorna. Don't worry if they contradict each other. Then have each person in your group find evidence in the text to support them. Discuss your findings as a group.

4. What is Lorna's attitude toward nature and religion? How do you know? (Give evidence from the text.) How is it different from the attitude of the "white people" she encounters? Discuss this with your group.

5. Write for a few minutes in your log about what you have learned from doing these activities.

HOW I READ IT

1. Reflect on making the time line in After Reading 2. How did it help you understand what you read? Can you think of another piece of reading you have done recently that this exercise could help you with?

2. With a partner, identify parts of this text that were easy to read and others that were difficult. Try to describe to each other what made them particularly difficult or easy.

3. List some words that you did not understand as you read the text for the first time. How did you come to understand these words?

Did you need to know all of these words in order to write about this piece? Explain in your reading log.

TOPICS FOR WRITING

1. Make a list of the things Lorna resents. Make another list of the things she loves. What can you say about her when you compare the two lists?

2. Choose one activity.

   Activity A: Describe Lorna's attitudes toward nature and technology. For example, why do you suppose Lorna rejects the snowmobile but embraces the airplane? What can we conclude from an analysis of her attitudes? Write a composition explaining how people like Lorna decide when it is appropriate to reject technology and when it is appropriate to accept it.

   Activity B: Lorna both resists changes and makes them. Have you ever known anyone like her? Using yourself or someone you know as an example, write a composition explaining how people like Lorna decide when it is appropriate to resist change and when it is appropriate to fight for change.

   Activity C: Go back to "The Journey" on p. 116. How is Lorna similar to the person in the poem? How is she different? Give examples from the text.

AFTER WRITING

1. Exchange papers with someone in the class that you have never talked to about your writing before. Respond in any way you wish.

2. Report to your group about what you learned from the new person you talked to that might be useful to the other group members.

BEFORE READING

1. Skim the piece: Read the title, subtitle, author's name, and the first sentence of each paragraph. Note the form used for the end of the essay.
2. In your log, write one statement you think Berry will make in his essay.

   Share your statement with your group and then with the class. Then read the whole piece.

Against PCs: Why I'm Not Going to Buy a Computer
Wendell Berry

Wendell Berry is an essayist, novelist, and poet who often writes about preserving our land and resources.

Like almost everybody else, I am hooked to the energy corporations, which I do not admire. I hope to become less hooked to them. In my work, I try to be as little hooked to them as possible. As a farmer, I do almost all of my work with horses. As a writer, I work with a pencil or a pen and a piece of paper.

My wife types my work on a Royal standard typewriter bought new in 1956, and as good now as it was then. As she types, she sees things that are wrong, and marks them with small checks in the margins. She is my best critic because she is the one most familiar with my habitual errors and weaknesses. She also understands, sometimes better than I do, what *ought* to be said. We have, I think, a literary cottage industry that works well and pleasantly. I do not see anything wrong with it.

A number of people, by now, have told me that I could greatly improve things by buying a computer. My answer is that I am not going to do it. I have several reasons, and they are good ones.

The first is the one I mentioned at the beginning. I would hate to think that my work as a writer could not be done without a direct dependence on strip-mined coal. How could I write conscientiously against the rape of nature if I were, in the act of writing, implicated in the rape? For the same reason, it matters to me that my writing is done in the daytime, without electric light.

I do not admire the computer manufacturers a great deal more than I admire the energy industries. I have seen their advertisements, attempting to seduce struggling or failing farmers into the belief that they can solve their problems by buying yet another piece of expensive equipment. I am familiar with their propaganda campaigns that have put computers into public schools that are in need of books. That computers are expected to become as common as TV sets in "the future" does not impress me or matter to me. I do not own a TV set. I do not see that computers are bringing us one step nearer to anything that does matter to me: peace, economic justice, ecological health, political honesty, family and community stability, good work.

What would a computer cost me? More money, for one thing, than I can afford, and more than I wish to pay to people whom I do not admire. But the cost would not be just monetary. It is well understood that technological innovation always requires the discarding of the "old model"—the "old model" in this case being not just our old Royal standard, but my wife, my critic, my closest reader, my fellow worker. Thus (and I think this is typical of present-day technological innovation), what would be superseded would be not only some thing, but some body. In order to be technologically up-to-date as a writer, I would have to sacrifice an association that I am dependent upon and that I treasure.

My final and perhaps my best reason for not owning a computer is that I do not wish to fool myself. I disbelieve, and therefore strongly resent, the assertion that I or anybody else could write better or more easily with a computer than with a pencil. I do not see why I should not be as scientific about this as the next fellow: When somebody has used a computer to write work that is demonstrably better than Dante's, and when this better is demonstrably attributable to the use of a computer, then I will speak of computers with a more respectful tone of voice, though I still will not buy one.

To make myself as plain as I can, I should give my standards for technological innovation in my own work. They are as follows:

1. The new tool should be cheaper than the one it replaces.
2. It should be at least as small in scale as the one it replaces.
3. It should do work that is clearly and demonstrably better than the one it replaces.
4. It should use less energy than the one it replaces.
5. If possible, it should use some form of solar energy, such as that of the body.

6. It should be repairable by a person of ordinary intelligence, provided that he or she has the necessary tools.

7. It should be purchasable and repairable as near to home as possible.

8. It should come from a small, privately owned shop or store that will take it back for maintenance and repair.

9. It should not replace or disrupt anything good that already exists, and this includes family and community relationships.

AFTER READING

1. Make a double entry in your log: On the left side of a page, write down two or three things Berry said that surprised or interested you. On the right side, write your feelings, thoughts, opinions, associations, questions, and so on.

   Share your writing with your group.

2. With a partner, make a list of the reasons Berry gives for not wanting to buy a computer.

   Share the list with your group. Then each person in the group should take one of the reasons and explain it fully to others in the group.

3. At the end of the essay, Berry says, "I should give my standards for technological innovation in my own work. They are as follows: . . ." What does he mean? What is the purpose of the nine points he lists next? Talk about this with your group.

4. A reader can learn a great deal about the character of a person by what the person writes. What kind of person do you think Wendell Berry is? Write a short description of him in your log. Support your impressions with references from his essay. Write for someone who has not read the essay.

   Share your writing with your group.

HOW I READ IT

1. How did skimming the piece before reading it help your reading? Talk about this with your group.

2. Share your findings with the class.

TOPICS FOR WRITING

1. Choose one activity.

   Activity A: Find one statement of Berry's that you strongly agree with or strongly disagree with. Write an essay stating your opinion and explaining why you think this way.

   Activity B: Think of a piece of modern technology that you do not wish to own. Write an essay called "Against _____: Why I Am Not Going to Buy a _____."

   Activity C: Berry's essay appeared in *Harper's* magazine. Write a letter to the magazine giving your reactions to the essay.

2. Save this piece.

3. Now read two of the letters in which readers responded to Berry's essay.

Letters

Wendell Berry's essay "Against PCs" provoked many letters from readers of Harper's. *Two of those letters appear here.*

Wendell Berry provides writers enslaved by the computer with a handy alternative: Wife—a low-tech energy-saving device. Drop a pile of hand-written notes on Wife and you get back a finished manuscript, edited while it was typed. What computer can do that? Wife meets all of Berry's uncompromising standards for technological innovation: she's cheap, repairable near home, and good for the family structure. Best of all, Wife is politically correct because she breaks a writer's "direct dependence on strip-mined coal."

History teaches us that Wife can also be used to beat rugs and wash clothes by hand, thus eliminating the need for the vacuum cleaner and washing machine, two more nasty machines that threaten the act of writing.

GORDON INKELES
Miranda, Calif.

The value of a computer to a writer is that it is a tool not for generating ideas but for typing and editing words. It is cheaper than a secretary (or a wife!) and arguably more fuel-efficient. And it enables spouses who are not inclined to provide free labor more time to concentrate on *their* own work.

We should support alternatives both to coal-generated electricity and to IBM-style technocracy. But I am reluctant to entertain alternatives that presuppose the traditional subservience of one class to another. Let the PCs come and the wives and servants go seek more meaningful work.

TOBY KOOSMAN
Knoxville, Tenn.

AFTER READING

1. a. Each group of four people should choose one letter, reread it, and restate the important points the writer makes.

   b. Split into two pairs, and find another pair that read the other letter. Make a new group of four. Explain to the other pair what the letter you read said.

2. Work with your partner. Write one sentence that expresses the main point of each letter.

   Are the main points of the two letters similar or different? (In other words, do Inkeles and Koosman agree or disagree?) Discuss this with the class.

BEFORE READING

1. Write down one thing you would say in a reply if you were Berry. Read it to your group.

2. Read Berry's reply.

Wendell Berry Replies

The foregoing letters surprised me with the intensity of the feelings they expressed. According to the writers' testimony, there is nothing wrong with their computers; they are utterly satisfied with them and all that they stand for. My correspondents are certain that I am wrong and that I am, moreover, on the losing side, a side already relegated to the dustbin of history. And yet they grow huffy and condescending over my tiny dissent. What are they so anxious about? . . .

I am also surprised by the meanness with which two of these writers refer to my wife. In order to imply that I am a tyrant, they suggest by both direct statement and innuendo that she is subservient, characterless, and stupid—a mere "device" easily forced to provide meaningless "free labor." I understand that it is impossible to make an adequate public defense of one's private life, and so I will only point out that there are a number of kinder possibilities that my critics have disdained to imagine: that my wife may do this work because she wants to and likes to; that she may find some use and some meaning in it; that she may not work for nothing. These gentlemen obviously think themselves feminists of the most correct and principled sort, and yet they do not hesitate to stereotype and insult, on the basis of one fact, a woman they do not know. They are audacious and irresponsible gossips. . . .

Finally, it seems to me that none of my correspondents recognizes the innovativeness of my essay. If the use of a computer is a new idea, then a newer idea is not to use one.

AFTER READING

1. Did Berry say any of the things you or your group members would have said? Write in your log for a few minutes.

2. With a partner, write a summary sentence of each paragraph of Berry's reply. Compare your sentences with those of others in your group. Share your findings with the class.

3. Which writer do you agree with most, Inkeles, Koosman, or Berry? Or do you agree with none of the three? Write for 10 minutes in your reading log.

   Read your writing to your group.

AFTER WRITING

1. Having read the two letters and Berry's reply, you can now reread with new eyes what you wrote for Topics for Writing after reading "Against PCs." Rewrite the piece with these possibilities in mind:

   You may want to add ideas.

   You may may want to take out, change, or reorder ideas.

   You may want to begin or end in a different way.

   You may want to rewrite the piece completely.

2. Pass your rewritten piece to others in your group. Attach a page to the paper on which group members can write a comment about the writing.

3. Write in your log about how you rewrote your piece. For example, what did you change? Why?

BEFORE READING

1. Read the introductory information to "The Future Is Yours (Still)." Then read the first sentence of each paragraph of the essay.

2. Write down one thing you understood from what you read. Share your writing with the class. Then read the passage.

The Future Is Yours (Still)
Abbie Hoffman

Serving as his own lawyer, Abbie Hoffman presented a closing argument in a district court in Massachusetts on April 15, 1987. He and 11 others were on trial for trespassing while protesting the recruiting of students by the CIA (Central Intelligence Agency) at the University of Massachusetts. The group was acquitted. This is part of Hoffman's statement.

When I was growing up in Worcester, Massachusetts, my father was very proud of democracy. He often took me to town-hall meetings in Clinton, Athol, and Hudson. He would say, See how the people participate, see how they participate in decisions that affect their lives—that's democracy. I grew up with the idea that democracy is not something you believe in, or a place you hang your hat, but it's something you do. You participate. If you stop doing it, democracy crumbles and falls apart. It was very sad to read last month that the New England town-hall meetings are dying off, and, in a large sense, the spirit of this trial is that grass-roots participation in democracy must not die. If matters such as we have been discussing here are left only to be discussed behind closed-door hearings in Washington, then we would cease to have a government of the people.

You travel around this country, and no matter where you go, people say, Don't waste your time, nothing changes, you can't fight the powers that be—no one can. You hear it a lot from young people. I hear it from my own kids: Daddy, you're so quaint to believe in hope. Kids today live with awful nightmares: AIDS will wipe us out; the polar ice cap will melt; the nuclear bomb will go off at any minute. Even the best tend to believe we are hopeless to affect matters. It's no wonder teenage suicide is at a record level. Young people are detached from history, the planet, and, most important, the future. I maintain to you that this detachment from the future, the lack of hope, and the high suicide rate among youth are connected. . . .

Thomas Paine, the most outspoken and farsighted of the leaders of the American Revolution, wrote long ago:

> Every age and generation must be as free to act for itself, in all cases, as the ages and generations which preceded it. Man has no property in man, neither has any generation a property in the generations which are to follow.

Thomas Paine was talking about this spring day in this courtroom. A verdict of not guilty will say, When our country is right, keep it right; but when it is wrong, right those wrongs. A verdict of not guilty will say to the University of Massachusetts that these demonstrators are reaffirming their rights as citizens who acted with justification. A verdict of not guilty will say what Thomas Paine said: Young people, don't give up hope. If you participate, the future is yours. Thank you.

AFTER READING

1. Reread the passage, choosing one of these activities:
   a. Annotate the passage. In your log, summarize your annotations or write a reaction to what you read.
   b. Make a double entry in your log.

   Share your writing with your group.

2. As a group, write one sentence summarizing Hoffman's main point. Discuss this sentence with the class.

TOPICS FOR WRITING

Choose one activity.

Activity A: Hoffman said, "Young people, don't give up hope. If you participate, the future is yours." But he also reported that many young people say, "Don't waste your time, nothing changes." Have you seen young people make changes in the world around them? Do you agree with Hoffman that young people can—and should—try to make positive changes in their society? Explain your opinion in writing, using your own experience and what you have seen and read to illustrate what you say.

Activity B: Hoffman and his colleagues protested against something they thought was wrong. Do you know of other people, either in this country or in other countries, who have done that? What were they protesting? How effective were the protests? Is "demonstrating" a good way to make change? Explain your opinion in writing, using your own experience and what you have seen and read to illustrate what you say.

Activity C: Think of a situation in your school, city, or country that you think is wrong. Make a list of ways in which you could let people know your ideas. Choose three or four of these ways, and write a composition describing and discussing them. Write this for someone who really wants to know how to go about suggesting a change.

AFTER WRITING

1. Attach a blank page to your paper. Pass the paper around so that one or two of your group members can write comments.

2. Read your readers' comments. Then read your writing to someone from another group.

BEFORE READING

1. Guess what answer you'll find in this passage to the implied question in "How Flowers Changed the World." Talk about it with a partner.

2. Read the introductory information and the passage.

How Flowers Changed the World
Loren Eiseley

This passage is from The Immense Journey, *Loren Eiseley's book about the evolution of life on the planet Earth, which began millions of years before humans appeared. Loren Eiseley is an anthropologist.*

Once upon a time there were no flowers at all.

A little while ago—about one hundred million years, as the geologist estimates time in the history of our four-billion-year-old planet—flowers were not to be found anywhere on the five continents. Wherever one might have looked, from the poles to the equator, one would have seen only the cold dark monotonous green of a world whose plant life possessed no other color.

Somewhere, just a short time before the close of the Age of Reptiles, there occurred a soundless, violent explosion. It lasted millions of years, but it was an explosion, nevertheless. It marked the emergence of the angiosperms—the flowering plants. Even the great evolutionist, Charles Darwin, called them "an abominable mystery," because they appeared so suddenly and spread so fast.

Flowers changed the face of the planet. Without them, the world we know—even man himself—would never have existed. Francis Thompson, the English poet, once wrote that one could not pluck a flower without troubling a star. Intuitively he had sensed like a naturalist the enormous interlinked complexity of life. Today we know that the appearance of the flowers contained also the equally mystifying emergence of man. . . .

A high metabolic rate and the maintenance of a constant body temperature are supreme achievements in the evolution of life. They enable an animal to escape, within broad limits, from the overheating or the chilling of its immediate surroundings, and at the same time to maintain a peak mental efficiency. Creatures without a high metabolic rate are slaves to weather. Insects in the first frosts of autumn all run down like little clocks. Yet if you pick one up and breathe warmly upon it, it will begin to move about once more. . . .

A high metabolic rate, however, means a heavy intake of energy in order to sustain body warmth and efficiency. It is for this reason that even some of these later warm-blooded mammals existing in our day have learned to descend into a slower, unconscious rate of living during the winter months when food may be difficult to obtain. On a slightly higher plane they are following the procedure of the cold-blooded frog sleeping in the mud at the bottom of a frozen pond.

The agile brain of the warm-blooded birds and mammals demands a high oxygen consumption and food in concentrated forms, or the creatures cannot long sustain themselves. It was the rise of the flowering plants that provided that energy and changed the nature of the living world. Their appearance parallels in a quite surprising manner the rise of the birds and mammals.

AFTER READING

1. In your log, write a short statement on how flowers changed the world. Share it with your partner and then with the class.

2. Choose and underline a sentence (or two) you like, for whatever reason. Read it to the class, and tell why you like it.

HOW IT'S WRITTEN

Although this passage is taken from a science book, it has features of poetry and storytelling as well as scientific writing. What features of writing do you generally associate with scientific writing? With poetry? With storytelling? With the class, put your findings on the chalkboard.

Look back through "How Flowers Changed the World," and find examples of words, sentences, or paragraphs in the passage that fit each category: scientific writing, poetry, storytelling.

TOPICS FOR WRITING

Choose one activity.

Activity A: Write a piece of your own, a true or imagined story or an essay titled "How _____ Changed the World." (You can change other words in the title if you want.)

Activity B: Choose a phrase or a sentence that strikes you as meaningful or gives you a topic. Use it to write a piece of your own. You might try **clustering, freewriting**, or **making a list** to get started (see Appendix A, p. 201).

Activity C: The passage says that a poet once wrote that "one could not pluck a flower without troubling a star." Eiseley says the poet was talking about the "interlinked complexity of life." If something happens to one thing, one person, one flower in the world, it has an effect on the rest of the world, even on a person thousands of miles away. Do you agree with that notion? Explain what you think as fully as you can.

AFTER WRITING

1. Read your writing aloud to your group. Ask group members to tell you what they understood your main point to be and what details stood out for them.

2. Choose one person from the group to report to the class a one- or two-sentence summary of what each person in the group wrote about.

3. In your log, write about how you wrote this piece. Was it easy or hard? What was the hardest part? The easiest part? Explain. Did the reading affect the way you wrote? If so, how?

BEFORE READING

1. Look at the words below and make up a "why" question, the kind of
   question people ask about life and change and adaptation. Use any
   of these words you like, and add others.

survive	search
change	know
brain	certainty
adapt	human
perfect	mammals
intelligence	life

   Share your question with your partner, and see if you can make up
   another question together.

2. Read the diary entry "December 4" by Hal Borland, which comes
   from his *Book of Days*.

December 4
Hal Borland

*Hal Borland, a writer and naturalist, was well known for his
editorials in* The New York Times *about the seasonal changes in
nature, like the arrival of spring.*

Change, I am told, is the one certainty of life. Change and adaptation
have been continuous.

I can accept that. But why, if change is inevitable, does the simplest
form of life, the form that presumably was among the very earliest in
existence on this earth, still persist? And if there is a ruthless weeding out of
the unfit and the weaklings, why did the insignificant primitive mammals
not perish through the 150 million years of big-lizard supremacy? Why did
man, a physical weakling even among the mammals, survive long enough
to perfect a big brain and his own dominant intelligence?

The persistent whys!

But, significantly, it is man himself, not the amoeba or the fish or the
lizard or the bird, who asks the questions. And that, ultimately, is the mark
of man—the search, the need to know, to understand.

AFTER READING

1. Write for a few minutes in your log about what you read:

   What did you understand?

   How do you feel about what you understood?

   What associations flow from your understanding?

   Look over what you wrote, and underline any sentences or phrases you like.

2. With a partner, look at the passage "December 4," and find three or four more words to add to the list of words in Before Reading.

3. With your partner, find the three questions Borland asks. How do those questions connect to the first paragraph?

   Talk about the connections with your partner.

HOW IT'S WRITTEN

The passage is taken from Borland's *Book of Days*. What do you think a "book of days" is? What characterizes this piece as a journal entry? How do you know it's not a story or a poem, for instance? With your partner, make a list of the features that tell you it is a journal entry. Look at your own log. See if your entries reflect similar features or reveal others.

TOPICS FOR WRITING

Choose one activity.

Activity A: People often say "The more things change, the more they stay the same." What does that mean to you? Would you say it or have you said it? When? Write a short piece about the statement and what it might apply to. Recount a relevant experience.

Activity B: Write a diary entry for today for yourself, starting with a statement about *change*. Title it with today's date.

Activity C: Borland says in the last paragraph, "But significantly it is man . . . who asks the questions," and asking questions is the mark of humans. Does our need to question, to engage in "the search, the need to know, to understand," relate to change? How? Can you think of things that have changed because of our need to search, know, and understand? Explain in writing.

AFTER WRITING

Exchange papers with the members of your group, and read each person's paper silently. Summarize in your log what the person is saying about change. Then share your thoughts with your group.

About All the Readings in This Chapter

PREPARING FOR WRITING

1. Reread all the entries in your reading log and all the writing you did for this chapter under Topics for Writing.

2. With a partner, choose one activity.

    Activity A: Some people accept and promote change; others resist it. Let's suppose the world needs both—the changers (for) and the resisters (against). Go back through all the readings in this chapter and categorize them according to attitudes toward change. Use the following categories, and add any of your own. (One piece, person, or writer may fit several categories.)

    Changers   *Resisters*

    Reasons for   *Reasons against*

    Benefits   *Drawbacks*

    Other categories

    Activity B: With your partner, make lists of all the technological equipment or innovations in your home, school, workplace, and recreation area. You can use those places as categories if you like. To help you, imagine how any of those places would be without electricity or batteries. Talk about what these things do for you and what life would be like without them. Which things could you do without? Which things do you absolutely need? Why?

Find a couple of other people in the class who have similar lists to yours. See what you have that they don't.

TOPICS FOR WRITING

Choose one activity.

Activity A: Have you ever proposed a change in your life or your family's life that other people have said no to? Have you ever said no to a change someone else has proposed? When? What happened? Write about such events. Give examples, and draw some conclusions.

Activity B: Reread the poem "First Grade" on p. 164. What people in other readings for this chapter have been in some way "unwilling to unlearn Old Ways"? What people have embraced new ways? Make two lists. Write a composition showing the differences and similarities between two people from one or both of your lists.

Activity C: Some people think it is better to bring children up in "natural" settings without a lot of technology, especially television and toys that run on batteries or electricity. They prefer that children build their own toys, develop their own games and activities, use their own physical energy to make their toys work, read books, and draw or create their own art. What do you think on this issue? Why? Write your thoughts on bringing up children in this technological age.

Activity D: Choose a piece you wrote for one of the readings in this chapter, and revise it in light of what you have learned from the other readings in the chapter.

AFTER WRITING

1. Go over your paper carefully with your pen in your hand, reading each word aloud so that your ear can hear it and touching each word with your pen to find errors and parts that don't sound right. Don't stop until you find at least three things to change.

2. Give your paper to at least two other people. Ask for written feedback on whatever you want help with.

3. Read your readers' comments. Then read what you wrote to your group. As a group, choose one piece to read to the class.

4. Look back in your log at all the writing you did about *how you wrote*. How has your writing process changed? For example, what do you do now (that you didn't use to do) to get started on a composition? To make your writing clearer? Discuss this with the class.

Extra Readings

Haiku
Teishitsu

The haiku, a 17-syllable verse form, has been used by Japanese poets for hundreds of years. A haiku is not a complete poem as we know it; rather it suggests a picture that readers are expected to fill in from their own imaginations.

Icicles and water
    Old differences dissolved . . .
Drip down together

Anishinabe Grandmothers
George Vizenor

The Anishinabe are a tribe of Native Americans.

anishinabe grandmothers
swelling like sweet clover on the dancing fields

stomachs swaying
print dresses smiling on the wind

tribal dream songs
coming from the past without teeth
more beautiful than flowers

dream children touching the earth again
with gnarled fingers

the scars of reservation life
turning under with age

the sacred earth remembers
every flower

grandchildren following
clumsy and clover stained
tasting the rain
singing
the world will change

Interview with a Lemming
James Thurber

A lemming is a mouselike rodent that lives in the Arctic tundra or meadows. Measuring about 5 inches long, it has a stout body with fluffy fur. Every three or four years, the lemming population becomes so large that the animals have to go long distances to find food, even swimming bodies of water in their frantic search. Folklore pictures lemmings committing mass suicide by plunging over cliffs or jumping into the ocean. The humorist James Thurber used this legend as the basis of his "Interview with a Lemming."

The weary scientist, tramping through the mountains of northern Europe in the winter weather, dropped his knapsack and prepared to sit on a rock.

"Careful, brother," said a voice.

"Sorry," murmured the scientist, noting with some surprise that a lemming which he had been about to sit on had addressed him. "It is a source of considerable astonishment to me," said the scientist, sitting down beside the lemming, "that you are capable of speech."

"You human beings are always astonished," said the lemming, "when any other animal can do anything you can. Yet there are many things animals can do that you cannot, such as stridulate, or chirr, to name just one. To stridulate, or chirr, one of the minor achievements of the cricket, your species is dependent on the intestines of the sheep and the hair of the horse."

"We are a dependent animal," admitted the scientist.

"You are an amazing animal," said the lemming.

"We have always considered you rather amazing, too," said the scientist. "You are perhaps the most mysterious of creatures."

"If we are going to indulge in adjectives beginning with 'm,'" said the lemming, sharply, "let me apply a few to your species—murderous, maladjusted, maleficent, malicious and muffle-headed."

"You find our behavior as difficult to understand as we do yours?"

"You, as you would say, said it," said the lemming. "You kill, you mangle, you torture, you imprison, you starve each other. You cover the nurturing earth with cement, you cut down elm trees to put up institutions for people driven insane by the cutting down of elm trees, you—"

"You could go on all night like that," said the scientist, "listing our sins and our shames."

"I could go on all night and up to four o'clock tomorrow afternoon," said the lemming. "It just happens that I have made a lifelong study of the self-styled higher animal. Except for one thing, I know all there is to know about you, and singularly dreary, dolorous and distasteful store of information it is, too, to use only adjectives beginning with 'd.'"

"You say you have made a lifelong study of my species—" began the scientist.

"Indeed I have," broke in the lemming. "I know that you are cruel, cunning and carnivorous, sly, sensual and selfish, greedy, gullible and guileful—"

"Pray don't wear yourself out," said the scientist, quietly. "It may interest you to know that I have made a lifelong study of lemmings, just as you have made a lifelong study of people. Like you, I have found but one thing about my subject which I do not understand."

"And what is that?" asked the lemming.

"I don't understand," said the scientist, "why you lemmings all rush down to the sea and drown yourselves."

"How curious," said the lemming. "The one thing I don't understand is why you human beings don't."

Appendix A

Gathering Ideas

1. FREEWRITING

Freewriting is one way of responding to what you read. It is also a way of unlocking ideas for writing.

Freewriting is writing without stopping for a certain period of time about a reading, topic, or question. When ideas stop coming, you simply write, "I can't think of anything to write" until a new idea comes into your mind. When freewriting, you should not be critical. Don't worry about things like spelling, grammar, or punctuation. Don't worry if ideas seem out of order or unrelated. Once you start writing, you just keep on writing until the time is up.

Figures 1 and 2 show the freewriting of two students about the words *leaving* and *arriving*.

After you freewrite, you may want to write one sentence that summarizes or states the most important thing you said in your writing. We call this important idea the *kernel*, the nucleus or core, of what you wanted to say.

Once you have a kernel sentence, you can freewrite on that sentence, and so on, until you get tired or until you think you've exhausted the subject. Or you can stop with one freewrite and read over what you've written to discover what you think and feel about a reading, topic, or question and to get ideas for more writing.

LOOPING

If you don't have much time and you don't want to write off the topic, which can happen with freewriting, and you have to come up with an idea on a specific topic for a writing assignment, you can try *looping*. Looping

Figure 1

Leaving. When I'm leaving from a place I get very sad, because I dont like to leave from a place that I love too much I want to tell you about my experience When I came from Santo Domingo it was a difficult time for me, because I let the people that I loved, my customs. my neibord. Also my animals such as my dog, my doves, and my cat. and I loved all of this. That the reason, why I said that it is hard leaving the place where you was born, and the place where you grew up. But arriving it also very nice, and sometimes very hard because you get to a place where you don't know anyone, you don't know where to go.

Damaris Ovalle

combines freewriting and kernel sentences. It is useful for finding your ideas on a given topic without losing a lot of time.

To do looping, you need a topic, even if it's unspecific and broad. Put the topic at the top of the page. Then freewrite without stopping for 5 to 10 minutes on the topic. Before starting, decide on the amount of time you can spend, and check the clock or set a timer. Stop when the time is up. Read over what you have written, and determine the main thing you seem to be talking about, the most important thing. Don't summarize. Pick out the main thing you want to say, and write a sentence stating that. It doesn't have to be what you wrote the most about. It can be something you like or even something you didn't quite say but want to. It is like a kernel sentence.

Now do another loop, using the sentence you wrote at the end of the first loop as the first sentence of the second loop. Time yourself again. Stop. Read what you wrote. Decide what the main thing was in what you just wrote, and write a sentence. Use that second sentence to start your third loop. Repeat the process one more time so that you have three loops.

Figure 2

Leave and arrive means to me, to reach a place and to get out of the place or sometimes leaving a place for ever whe For Example I am leaving New York next month. Here the meaning is like extend the time. leaving sounds like a big word or when you take all your thin personal things with you. Leaving sound at to me depressed.

Arrive or arriving it has a happy expectation is like waiting for somebody at the airport and the time pass slowly and we are anxious because to see that person. Sometimes arriving makes me feel sick it happened when I went to visited my sister to florida my stomach was deep in I felt a like big heavy stone in my stomach then after arriving the airport all this symtoms of arrive were gone Leaving and arriving have a very classic sound it reminds me a (English) Brithis movie or sometimes at Channel 13.

Gilena Guevara

By this time, you will probably find that you have an idea that you can develop into a longer piece of writing.

2. CLUSTERING

Clustering or *making a map* can be done before you read, after you read, or before you write. It's one way of gathering ideas about a topic.

Clustering can be done with a group or by yourself. When it's done with the class, the instructor (or a student) starts by writing the topic in the middle of the chalkboard. Students then suggest words or phrases they associate with the topic, and the instructor writes them on the board around the topic. If the instructor or other students don't understand the relationship between the words suggested and the topic, the speaker explains it. You'll find that doing clustering with a group will often make you think of associations you might not think of on your own.

To cluster on your own, you start by writing the topic in the middle of a page in your reading log. Then you let your mind move out from the central topic in different directions. You quickly write down any word or idea that comes to you, connecting it to the previous word with a line. When a different idea comes to your mind, one unrelated to a previous word, you begin a new branch off the main topic. When you're finished, your page will have a design or a map of all your ideas.

Clustering allows the mind to bring forth ideas and thought patterns you might not see if you were simply writing. Because you splash down thoughts spontaneously, without judging their logic or appropriateness, you can often come up with new and creative ideas and relationships.

Figure 3 shows one class's cluster (map) around the title "Leaving Home Behind."

3. MAKING A LIST

Making a list can sometimes help you collect your ideas on a topic. You start by writing the topic at the top of your paper; underneath it, you list whatever words or phrases come to you. Just as with clustering or freewriting, it's important to let your mind flow without interruption, without being critical of what you put down. In other words, don't reject any idea that comes to mind. You will have a chance to select later. When you run out of ideas on the topic, you stop writing.

Figure 3

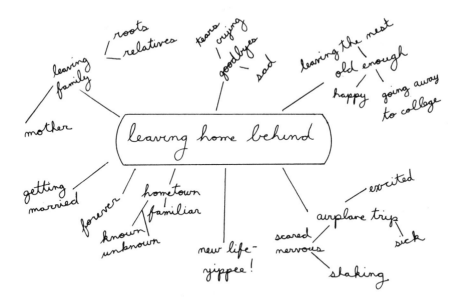

Figure 4 shows one person's listing about what she expected before she came to New York City and what she found when she got there.

Brainstorming a list can also be done with a group or the class. One person records all the ideas other students suggest in response to a topic. Group brainstorming is a good way to generate a lot of ideas on a topic. Often someone else's idea can prompt a new idea from you, one you might not have thought of on your own.

Once you have a list of ideas, it's easy to read them over, pick out those that are most closely related to the topic, and cross out those that aren't suitable. If you wish, you can put the remaining ideas into categories or groups, or you can draw arrows connecting things that go together. You may find that one idea can be a heading for one of your categories. Or you might find that one idea is a good central focus for what you want to write about. You may even want to make another list using one of the ideas on your original list as the new topic.

Making a list of events in a story, for example, can also help you put things in the order in which they happened or the order in which you want to present them. Then, when you start writing the story, you have a guide for what to write about next.

Figure 4

What I expected	What I found
streets of gold	dirty streets
friends	crowds, people everywhere
weather like my country	snow, cold
my language	my language <u>and</u> English
nice people	new friends - later
tall buildings	people in a hurry,
Statue of Liberty	sometimes rude
job	taller buildings than
to be free to do what	I imagined
I want	poor people - <u>many</u>
Fifth Avenue	not complete
beautiful clothes	freedom

Getting Started
Robert M. Pirsig

In this excerpt from Zen and the Art of Motorcycle Maintenance *by Robert M. Pirsig, Chris's father gives him advice on how to use listing in order to start a letter to his mother.*

This road keeps on winding down through this canyon. Early morning patches of sun are around us everywhere. The cycle hums through the cold air and mountain pines and we pass a small sign that says a breakfast place is a mile ahead.

"Are you hungry?" I shout.

"Yes!" Chris shouts back.

Soon a second sign saying CABINS with an arrow under it points off to the left. We slow down, turn and follow a dirt road until it reaches some varnished log cabins under some trees. We pull the cycle under a tree, shut off the ignition and gas and walk inside the main lodge. The wooden floors have a nice clomp under the cycle boots. We sit down at a tableclothed table and order eggs, hot cakes, maple syrup, milk, sausages and orange juice. That cold wind has worked up an appetite.

"I want to write a letter to Mom," Chris says.

That sounds good to me. I go to the desk and get some of the lodge stationery. I bring it to Chris and give him my pen. That brisk morning air has given him some energy too. He puts the paper in front of him, grabs the pen in a heavy grip and then concentrates on the blank paper for a while.

He looks up. "What day is it?"

I tell him. He nods and writes it down.

Then I see him write, "Dear Mom:"

Then he stares at the paper for a while.

Then he looks up. "What should I say?"

I start to grin. I should have him write for an hour about one side of a coin. I've sometimes thought of him as a student but not as a rhetoric student.

We're interrupted by the hot cakes and I tell him to put the letter to one side and I'll help him afterward.

When we are done I sit smoking with a leaden feeling from the hot cakes and the eggs and everything and notice through the window that under the pines outside the ground is in patches of shadow and sunlight.

Chris brings out the paper again. "Now help me," he says.

"Okay," I say. I tell him getting stuck is the commonest trouble of all. Usually, I say, your mind gets stuck when you're trying to do too many things at once. What you have to do is try not to force words to come. That just gets you more stuck. What you have to do now is separate out the things and do them one at a time. You're trying to think of what to *say* and what to say *first* at the same time and that's too hard. So separate them out. Just make a list of all the things you want to say in any old order. Then later we'll figure out the right order.

"Like what things?" he asks.

"Well, what do you want to tell her?"

"About the trip."

"What things about the trip?"

He thinks for a while. "About the mountain we climbed."

"Okay, write that down," I say.

He does.

Then I see him write down another item, then another, while I finish my cigarette and coffee. He goes through three sheets of paper, listing things he wants to say.

"Save those," I tell him, "and we'll work on them later."

"I'll never get all this into one letter," he says.

He sees me laugh and frowns.

I say, "Just pick out the best things." Then we head outside and onto the motorcycle again.

---

4. CUBING

Cubing is a good way to look at a person, an object, a feeling, or an idea from six different perspectives. Like a cube, the writing you do while cubing has six sides (see Figure 5 below). You should write quickly, spending 3 to 5 minutes on each side of your cube.

Here's what you do on each side of your cube:

1. *Describe it*: What does it look like? What are its characteristics? What are the first things you notice about it?

2. *Compare it*: What is it similar to? What is it different from?

3. *Associate it*: What does it remind you of? How does it connect with your individual life, with the life of your family or community?

4. *Analyze it*: Look deeper. What is it really made of? How does it work?

5. *Apply it*: What is it used for? Who uses it?

6. *Argue for it or against it*: Is it a good thing or a bad one? Explain why.

When you are finished, read what you wrote, and put a star beside one or two of the six small pieces of writing you did that seem most powerful or most interesting to you or that you would like to develop further. Freewrite about them again.

Figure 5

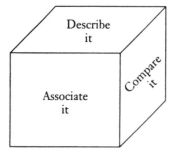
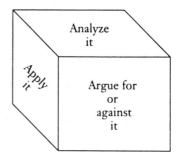

Appendix B

Responding to Readings

---

1. RESPONSE QUESTIONS

Rather than writing freely in response to a reading, you may sometimes want guidance. These three questions in this order are a useful guide:

1. What did you perceive (notice, remember) in what you read? What did you understand the reading to be about?

2. How do you feel about what you understood or saw? What is your opinion of what you read (or of one part of what you read)?

3. What associations flow from your thoughts and feelings? What does it remind you of in your own life or in the lives of people you know or in other reading you have done?

Figure 6 shows the answers one student, Félix Marie Félix, wrote to these three questions after reading "Leaving Home Behind."

Figure 6

1. What do you understand?

For many people the realization of their dream is to leave their country and come to U.S. But it was frustration and pain for Melba Cruz. She planned to leave home early because the goodbyes of her kids seemed as "you are running away from us." But they woke up early dressed up and waitting for her at the front door of the house to say goodbye.

She looked sadly at their innocent faces. She had to go they kissed and hugged her and said goodbye.

2. How do you feel about what you understand?

In my own experience I think it's really very hard to leave your country. It's more hard when you left your relatives behind specially your mother. I feel how she felt because she have to leave her kids she didn't like to come to U. S.

3. What do you associate with your understanding?

Come to U. S. was frustration and pain for her. I think I felt the same way with her when I had to come to U. S. I didn't really feel coming to U. S. I had to live with my father who I didn't know very well. While I left my mother in my country I had a very hard time but I must come to help my mother and my brother behind.

2. DOUBLE-ENTRY NOTEBOOK

A *double-entry notebook* is a special reading log. It allows you to note points in your reading that interest you and then to talk with yourself about them. Here is how it works.

Draw a line down the middle of one page of your notebook. As you read a passage or after you finish reading it, on the left side of your notebook page, jot down interesting or important words, phrases, sentences, ideas, points, details, and the like. You can write down the exact words as they appear in the text (*quote*), you can say the ideas in your own words (*paraphrase*), or you can *summarize*, in your own words, important or interesting ideas or main events from the passage. Then, on the right side of your notebook page, write your own comments about the material you put on the left side. You can question; react; express confusion; connect; relate to other reading or your own experience; make observations about your reading process; express your feelings, thoughts, and ideas; and so on.

Left Side	**Right Side**
interesting/important quotes/paraphrases:	your comments:
words	ideas
phrases	questions
sentences	reactions
ideas	confusions
points	connections
details	feelings
	thoughts

Figure 7 shows what Taunys Almanzar wrote in her double-entry notebook after reading "Freedom."

Taunys wrote a two-sentence summary of the major events of the story on the left side of her notebook page. On the right side of the page, she wrote several kinds of comments:

Reaction ("I think this story is very sad," "hard to believe")

Questions ("What was really happening in China?" "Why was he trying to escape?")

Another reader, of course, will note different things and have different reactions to the story simply because each reader's knowledge and experiences are unique.

Figure 7

Freedom

This story is about a
China guy who was try
to escape from his
country. Finally, he
did it, but the Hong
Kong policeman caught
him and took back
to China.

I think this story
is very sad. Its hard
to believe how those
people in China were try
to escape. What was
really happend in
China? Why him was
try to escape?

Figure 8 shows an entry from Maria Collado's double-entry notebook. She, too, read and commented on "Freedom."

Maria, too, summarized the major events as she understood them on the left side of her notebook page. On the right, she wrote two kinds of comments:

Reaction ("a sad story")

Personal association ("it was like . . . the story of the people from my country")

You can see that each reader found different ways of relating to the story. The value of writing your *own* understanding and your *own* comments about what you read is that it helps you enrich your reading by deepening your understanding of what you read and relating to it personally. In other words, there is no right answer; you notice what's important to *you*, and you react and respond from *yourself*.

An additional enrichment can come when you share your notebooks with other readers. Reading (and then talking about) other people's interpretations of a text will broaden your understanding of that text. Other readers' reactions and associations help you see the text in new ways. For

Figure 8

The story was about someone who was trying to escape from his country, Mainland China, to Hong Kong. He was very excited because he thought that he had made it, but, when he arrived to Hong Kong, his dream was shattered, by policeman that was waiting for him to take him back to China.

For me it was a sad story because while I was reading, I was imaging it was like if I was reading the story of all the people from my country, the Dominican Republic, who every day are trying to escape from the poverty of our country, and many time they had had more bad luck than this student had because there had been time in which they are being killed.

these reasons, this book often asks you to share your notebook entries with other students, usually in small groups.

FOUR-ENTRY NOTEBOOK

Instead of talking aloud to someone about your double-entry responses, you can have a "conversation in writing" in a four-entry notebook. Here's how it works.

Draw a line down a right-hand page of your notebook across from a left-hand page on which you've made a double entry. Now you have four columns.

Pass your notebook to another person. This person reads your double entry and writes a response in the third column. After that, you have several choices:

1. You can take your notebook back, read your partner's response, and write a response to that in the fourth column on the right half of the page.

2. Another student or your instructor can take your notebook and, in the fourth column on the right half of the page, write a response to all the writing on those two pages of your log.

Whichever option you choose, a "conversation in writing" takes place among two or three people about your reading of a text.

Figure 9 shows an example of a four-entry notebook. Columns 1 and 2 contain Taunys Almanzar's double-entry response to "Notes on Being a Foreigner." Column 3 shows Nora Uceda's response to what Taunys wrote, and column 4 shows the instructor's response.

3. ANNOTATING

Annotating is a way of reading with a pencil in hand. As you read, you mark up the text in any way that makes sense to you:

Underline, circle, or bracket important or interesting words, phrases, and sentences.

Draw arrows to connect related ideas.

Write comments and questions in the margins.

Number points.

Make any other markings that are meaningful to you.

Don't be shy about making marks on the text! If you don't want to write directly on the text, you can write on a photocopy or make the same kinds of notes in your notebook.

Most people who annotate read a text several times and make more annotations each time they read it. Rereading helps them see things in a new way and with fresh understanding.

Figure 10 shows one student's annotations on "Notes on Being a Foreigner."

Figure 9

"Cities flow on, like water, and, like water, they close behind any departure."

- hostile
- aggressive
- overfriendly
- distant
- possession

I like this sentence and these words. I read this article two times and I can't see clearly what is his main point. I already know that he is talking about his experience as a foreigner because he is a writer. But I really don't understand very well his words. Maybe if he express himself by real examples I could understand his point more.

I suggest if the writer of this book use other details that may support more strongly his ideas, it would be easy to understand

Taunya:
I read it about five times and I couldn't see any main point. I understand everything like you but I can't express what I understand. I think this is difficult to understood.

I agree with you.

Nora

Taunya: Why do you like the sentence you wrote down? I like it, too. I think it's because it makes me picture a river flowing around a person. Maybe he meant that people arrive in and depart from cities, and the cities don't pay any attention.

Why do you like the other words you wrote down? Maybe Mr. Reid should take your suggestions about using other details to make his writing easier to understand!

Jean

Figure 10

Notes on Being a Foreigner

I come suddenly into a foreign city, just as the lamps take light along the water, with some notes in my head. Arriving—the mood and excitement, at least, are always the same. I try out the language with the taxi driver, to see if it is still there; and later, I walk to a restaurant that is lurking round a corner in my memory. Nothing, of course, has changed; but cities flow on, like water, and, like water, they close behind any departure. We come back to confirm them, even though they do not particularly care. Or perhaps we come back to confirm ourselves?

What does he want to find there again?

Who are "them"?

what does he mean?

*

[Natives feel oddly toward foreigners.] They may be hostile, aggressive, overfriendly, distant, or possessive; but at least they have the (to them) advantage of being in possession, so that between foreigners and themselves there is a moat with a drawbridge to which they keep the keys. Typical native gambits: "Why, we almost consider you one of us!" Or "What do you think of our (railways, king, public lavatories)?" Or "Are you familiar with our expression . . . ?" They have the assurance of Being In Possession.

?

?

?

That's what I meant when I said "relationship" about the title.

What's possession?

*

Kinds of foreigners:
1.) necessity
2.) accident
3.) choice

And the foreigner? It depends on whether he is a foreigner by Necessity, Accident, or Choice. One thing, however, is sure: unless he regards being a foreigner as a positive state, he is doomed. If he has already chosen not to belong, then all the native gambits are bound to fail. But if he aspires to being a native, then he is forever at the mercy of the natives, down to the last inflection of the voice.

?
?

?

Why is the foreigner forever at the mercy of the natives?

4. DESCRIPTIVE OUTLINING

The goal of the descriptive outline is to help you see a piece of writing more clearly and objectively. Descriptive outlining is a tool for revision and should be done between two drafts of a piece of writing.

Set up your descriptive outline this way:

Main idea:_____
>   Paragraph 1 says:_____
>   does:_____
>   Paragraph 2 says:_____
>   does:_____
>   Paragraph 3 says:_____
>   does:_____

For *main idea*, write the main idea of the composition, either as it is stated by the writer or in your own words.

For what each paragraph *says*, write a one-sentence summary of the paragraph.

For what each paragraph *does*, explain the function of the paragraph in the composition. That is, what is the work the writer intends it to accomplish in the composition? A paragraph can do many things. It can present an idea, give an example, give a reason, argue logically; it can analyze; it can explain; it can list and catalog objects, events, scenes, problems; it can tell a story; it can describe a person, place, or thing; it can compare; it can conclude. Paragraphs analyze, describe, and argue in order to help defend or explain the main point of the composition. When you tell what a paragraph *does*, you are telling how it develops the main idea.

DESCRIPTIVE OUTLINING EXAMPLE

"Private Language" by Patty Crespo

Main idea (Paragraph 1): Immigrants should learn English to keep the United States united, but they should not exchange their own culture for an American way of life.

Paragraph 2 says: Immigrants need English in daily life and emergency situations, such as when they have to call the ambulance.

does: Gives a reason and an example of why immigrants should learn English, the public language.

Paragraph 3 says: Immigrants should keep their native language in order to communicate with their relatives.

does: Gives a reason and an example of why immigrants should not forget their native language.

Paragraph 4 says: Immigrants can replace their language with English, but the Constitution of the United States gives them the right to keep and transmit their cultural values to future generations.

does: Argues that immigrants have the right to keep their cultural traditions.

Paragraph 5 says: Immigrants should learn English to communicate with the public and keep the country united but have the right to keep their culture and transmit it to future generations.

does: Concludes the composition by restating the main idea and the idea in paragraph 4.

Appendix C

The Reading Process (How We Read)

A number of times in this book, you'll be asked to reflect on *how* you read a passage, that is, on your reading process. Becoming aware of the reading strategies you already use and learning some new ones from your classmates and from the activities in this book will help you to become a better, more fluent reader.

In response to the How I Read It activity on p. 27, students in one class described a variety of strategies they used when reading "Worlds to Go before I Sleep." These were some of the strategies they mentioned.

It was difficult because of the vocabulary, so I read it quickly the first time, and then slowly the second time. I tried to figure out the meaning of the hard words from the sentences around them.

I read it slowly and tried to understand the meaning of every word.

I underlined words I didn't know and then later, at home, looked them up in the dictionary.

I used a dictionary for words I didn't know.

I didn't use a dictionary because it would take too long.

When I couldn't understand a word, I looked at the rest of the sentence and the paragraph to see if I could get the meaning from the context.

I reread parts I didn't understand.

I skipped things and words I didn't understand.

I asked questions. Then sometimes, when I read more of the story, I could answer my questions.

It was hard because of all the "I," "I," "I." I didn't know who was telling the story. I had to try to figure that out.

I read it two or three times. I understood it better then.

Appendix D

The Writing Process (How We Write)

In this book, you'll be asked to reflect on *how* you wrote your composition, that is, on your writing process. Your writing process is a complex activity, like playing soccer or dancing. You can develop it by learning and practicing certain skills and strategies: for example, learning ways of getting started, like freewriting or clustering; sharpening your observation skills; writing faster and longer; rewriting; and editing. You can learn new strategies by reflecting on what you do as you write and by watching or talking to other people about how they write.

Here are some examples of what several students said about *how* they wrote on the Topics for Writing, p. 28, after reading "Worlds to Go before I Sleep." In After Writing 3, p. 28, they were told: "Write in your log about *how* you wrote this composition (your process of writing)." Their responses give you an idea of their writing process.

First, I started doing freewriting to build up my idea. . . . I wrote it three times: First I took out the freewriting that I did. Then I checked which sentences I could keep, the ideas, many details, and so on. That was my first draft. Then I rewrote it because I thought about new words, new sentences, and I had to add more paragraphs. And the final draft, that is the one I am giving to you. That I think is perfect and well done. (SANTA)

I decided to write about that topic because the little girl reminded me of the first time I came to America. . . . When I faced this topic I thought about it for two or three minutes . . . going back to the past and . . . to the present. I tried to remember how I felt the first time I knew I would be coming to America. I kept writing for 20 minutes. I wrote it twice, the second time I just . . . cut certain things. I did not change it. And then in the morning I reread it again and that's that. (MARIE)

I chose topic A because I can write more and in B and C there are specific questions. I wrote my composition two times, the first one here in the classroom, but I was not sure about some words and I changed some things. I added many things the second time. I had an idea here but I didn't know how to write it in English and wrote it in Spanish and I translated it at home. (NORA)

I wrote my composition about my feelings when I came to New York. I took around two hours because I rewrote it two times. I changed a lot of words and tried to organize my ideas and the meaning of each word. (FABIOLA)

It takes a long time to learn to write. Don't get impatient, but be reflective and watchful. The more you add strategies like the ones that these student writers used to your own writing process, the more prepared you will be to meet future writing assignments.

Appendix E

After Writing

Each After Writing section has two types of activities: sharing your writing and giving feedback (or responding) to your classmates' writing, and reflecting on how you wrote (your writing process). (Reflecting on your writing process is discussed in Appendix D. Look there for examples and discussion.)

You'll be asked to *share your writing* with your classmates, either by exchanging papers and reading silently or by reading your piece aloud. After you read or listen to your classmates' writing, you're asked to *give a response or feedback* based on questions or guidelines provided. Sometimes you'll do this in a group, sometimes with a partner and occasionally you'll be asked to give yourself feedback on your own writing.

The questions are about things any reader or listener can respond to about a piece of writing. They are not technical. That is, you are not expected to give feedback as an editor or a teacher. You don't have to give suggestions for revision or make corrections. Simply be yourself as an active reader or listener, and say something to the writer. Use the questions as guidelines.

Here are a few examples of the kinds of questions you'll be asked to respond to in After Writing:

Tell what you like about the composition.

Restate (or retell) what you understood.

What details stand out for you, the reader?

What point does this piece make?

How could this piece of writing be improved?

What examples does the writer include?

Do the examples illustrate the writer's point?

How does the writer develop the point (idea)?

Some of the terms used in these After Writing questions may not be familiar to you at first. But you can understand them in their commonsense meanings. If you don't understand certain ones, discuss them with your instructor and classmates. Try to use the words as you think they mean. They will become clearer as you go along. Remember, there are no right or wrong answers.

A few terms used frequently in the After Writing questions are defined here briefly. The reading passages throughout the book contain many examples of each. If you discuss these terms with your instructor and classmates, look back at some of the readings for examples.

point: central idea; what the writer is trying to say; the message; the lesson; may be implied or stated explicitly.

example: a story, an experience, or other specifics used to illustrate a point.

detail: a bit of added information, often sensory (visual, auditory, related to touch or feeling, etc.).

development: how the writer starts, builds, and concludes an idea or a point throughout a piece of writing.

The following composition was written by a student in response to Topics for Writing on p. 19. Several students' responses, based on the questions that follow the student writing, may give you an idea of how you can respond to your classmates' writing.

As a foreigner I really appreciate Linda Yu's idea that the Americans don't welcome new people, new ideas and so on because I've experienced remarks and gestures that let me understand that I wasn't welcome in the U.S.

One day, while working with a few American and [West Indian] colleagues, a radio was on when a bulletin was published about a revolution among the people in Haiti, protesting against the Tonton Macoute's regime. I've always been well regarded among my colleagues and nothing has ever let me see hard feelings towards me. That day, after the bulletin, one of my women colleagues said, "I don't know why they don't stay in their country. Our America is getting to be overcrowded because people from everywhere are fleeing their country to find something better here and us Americans, we are losing our jobs to them. They are eating our food and taking away our apartments. Why don't they stay in their country and fight for their freedom instead of coming here?" Then I answered her, "Foreigners are not taking anything from you because they work hard for all they got." She did not agree with me.

In conclusion, America may very well be a melting pot, but all of us do not really melt sometimes. They make us really feel as outsiders. The discrimination is almost everywhere—Whites for Blacks, among Blacks for Hispanic and West Indians. The melting pot is boiling over flowing by sending most of the foreigners over the rim.   (JULES FRANTZ JEAN)

AFTER WRITING EXAMPLE

Write a response to this composition using the following questions to guide you:

    a. What point does this piece make? Is it clear?
    b. What do you like about this writing?

    a.   The rejection towards us. They make us feel as outsiders. . . . They think we taking away their thing, apartment, job. . . . We aren't taking their job, food, etc. Just we try to find another life style, something better for us.
    b.   I'm agree with this, show the way we feel the discrimination against us. . . .   (FELIX ANDRES LEROUX)

    a.   This piece points about how a foreigner feels in the U.S.A. It's not clear because all the people has different opinions, I mean the foreigner people.
    b.   My personal opinion it's that the American welcome the foreigner people, if we are working people and produce for this country.
(GIOCONDA CORDERO)

    a.   This piece let me believe that American people is unhappy to see a foreigner come to his country. It's why this Haitian student doesn't agree with those women by saying to them: "Foreigners are not taking anything from you because they work hard for all they got."
    b.   I like the way the Haitian student answers his women colleagues. (JOSSELYN FENELON)

By sharing your writing and giving responses, like these students', you'll get a sense of how others hear you. You can learn to make your ideas clear to your peers. They are an important audience. As you learn to write so that they understand, you will become a much stronger writer than you were before.

Acknowledgments (continued from p. iv)

Page 50, Lardas, Konstantinos, trans. "Exile and Orphanhood and Bitterness and Love." *Mourning Songs of Greece*, published in *College English*, Vol. 49, No. 1 (January, 1987), p. 40. Copyright 1987 by the National Council of Teachers of English. Reprinted with permission.

Page 52, Aslanian, Yeghia, "A Story of Conflicts," From *Hudson River, a Manhattan community journal*, EDN 27, Dec. 1987.

Page 57, Gornick, Vivian, Excerpt from *Fierce Attachments* by Vivian Gornick. Copyright © 1987 by Vivian Gornick. Reprinted by permission of Farrar, Straus and Giroux, Inc.

Page 62, Crespo, Patty (Jannette). "Private Language" by Patty Crespo.

Page 66, cummings, e.e. "old age sticks" is reprinted from *Complete Poems, 1913–1962*, by e. e. cummings, by permission of Liveright Publishing Corp. Copyright © 1923, 1924, 1925, 1931, 1935, 1938, 1939, 1940, 1944, 1945, 1946, 1947, 1948, 1949, 1950, 1951, 1952, 1953, 1954, 1955, 1956, 1957, 1958, 1959, 1960, 1961, 1962 by the trustees for the e. e. cummings Trust. Copyright © 1961, 1963, 1968, by Marion Morehouse Cummings.

Page 67, Santoli, Al, "Family Conflicts." From *New Americans* by Al Santoli. Copyright © Al Santoli, 1988. All rights reserved. Reprinted by permission of Viking Penguin, a division of Penguin Books, USA, Inc.

Page 69, Cameron, Peter, "Homework" from *One Way or Another* by Peter Cameron. Copyright © 1986 by the author. Reprinted by permission of Harper & Row, Inc.

Page 78, Excerpt from Ecclesiastes. Ecclesiastes 3:1–8, from the *New English Bible*, copyright 1971.

Page 81, Icaza, Jorge. "A Miraculous Event" by Jorge Icaza. *ESL Voices: Selections from ESL Students' Writing*, New York: Department of Developmental Skills, Borough of Manhattan Community College, CUNY, May, 1985.

Page 84, Simon, Kate. From *Bronx Primitive* by Kate Simon. All rights reserved. Reprinted by permission of Viking Penguin, a division of Penguin Books, USA, Inc.

Page 90, Kenney, Susan. *In Another Country* by Susan Kenney. Copyright © 1975, 1980, 1984 by Susan Kenney. All rights reserved. Reprinted by permission of Viking Penguin, a division of Penguin Books, USA, Inc.

Page 93, Paley, Grace. "Mother" from *Later the Same Day* by Grace Paley. Copyright © 1985 by Grace Paley. Reprinted by permission of Farrar, Straus & Giroux, Inc.

Page 98, Inouye, Yasushi. From *Chronicle of My Mother* published by Kodansha International Ltd. © 1982. Reprinted by permission. All rights reserved.

Page 103, Thomas, Lewis. From *The Lives of a Cell* by Lewis Thomas. Copyright © 1974 by Lewis Thomas. All rights reserved. Reprinted by permission of Viking Penguin, a division of Penguin Books, USA, Inc.

Page 109, Buddha, "Now May Every Living Thing." From *The Oxford Book of Prayer*.

Page 110, "One Is Born, One Dies" (African Proverb) from *African Proverbs*, p. 29., by Charlotte and Wolf Leslau, © 1962. Reprinted by permission of Peter Pauper Press.

Page 110, Carver, Raymond. "What the Doctor Said." From the book *A New Path to the Waterfall*, by Raymond Carver. Copyright © 1989 by the estate of Raymond Carver. Used by permission of Atlantic Monthly.

Page 111, "How the Milky Way Came to Be" (African folk tale) from *African Folk Tales* p. 56 by Charlotte and Wolf Leslau. Copyright 1963. By permission of Peter Pauper Press.

Page 111, Dipo, Beverly. "No Rainbows, No Roses" by Beverly Dipo. Copyright © 1986 by St. Martin's Press, Inc. From *Student Writers at Work: The Bedford Prizes* by Nancy Sommers and Donald McQuade. Reprinted by St. Martin's Press, Inc.

Page 115, "Peanuts" cartoon by Charles Schultz. March 28, copyright 1989 by United Feature Syndicate. Reprinted by permission of United Feature Syndicate, Inc.

Page 116, Oliver, Mary. From the book *Dream Work* by Mary Oliver, copyright © 1986 by Mary Oliver. Used by permission of the Atlantic Monthly Press.

Page 120, Anzaldúa, Gloria. "Tlilli, Tlapalli: The Path of the Red and Black Ink" from *Borderlands/La Frontera* © Gloria Anzaldua 1987, Spinsters/Aunt Lute Book Company, P.O. Box 410687, San Francisco, CA 94141.

Page 123, Plath, Sylvia. "Reflections of a Seventeen-Year-Old" from *Letters Home* by Sylvia Plath. Copyright © 1975 by Aurelia Shober Plath.

Page 127, Hungry Wolf, Adolf and Beverly. "Young Hunter of Picuris" p. 29. (Under the title 'Growing Up Outdoors: Young Hunter' from *Children of the Sun*, by Adolf and Beverly Hungry Wolf. By permission of William Morrow & Co., Inc.

Page 130, de Jesus, Carolina Maria. *Child of the Dark: The Diary of Carolina Maria de Jesus.* Translation from the Portuguese by David St. Clair. English translation 1962, E. P. Dutton Co., Inc. New York: Signet paperback, New American Library, 1963.

Illustration Credits

Page 1, © Carl Glassman/The Image Works. All rights reserved.
Page 44, © Deborah Kahn Kalas, Stock, Boston, 1988.
Page 114, © Jack Spratt/The Image Works.
Page 162, © Bill Coleman, State College, PA.
Cover Art: *Souvenir de Mauve*, Vincent van Gogh, Kröller-Müller Stichting.

Index